MAN'S DESIRE FOR GOD

BY

Fr. Brian Mullady, O.P., S.T.D.

ISBN: 1-4033-9933-6 (e-book)
ISBN: 1-4033-9934-4 (Paperback)

Library of Congress Control Number: 2002116348

This book is printed on acid free paper.

Printed in the United States of America
Bloomington, IN

1stBooks - rev. 02/13/03

ACKNOWLEDGEMENTS

Thanks are due to George Curran and his niece Anne Barthel for their help with the editing of this book. Without their encouragement, this book could never have been published. Also, to Fr. Reginald Martin, O.P. whose delightful initial editing gave hope to the author that someone would really appreciate the work and thus stimulated his courage to finish the book.

I also wish to acknowledge the many turns of phrase and references I used in the composition of the latter half of Chapter Three on fatherhood taken from the delightful book by Clayton Barbeau, The Head of the Family, long out of print. They are too many to be cited in the chapter. The quote from Homer in this same chapter comes from Dr. Conrad Baars, Psychic Wholeness and Healing, another great influence on my thinking. Many thanks to both.

DEDICATION

To Fr. Quintin Turiel, O.P., whose vast knowledge of St. Thomas was the inspiration and whose ideas form much of the foundation for this book. AD MULTOS ANNOS! And to the Dominican students of the Province of the Holy Name of Jesus whose supernatural orientation gives much hope for the future.

Table of contents

INTRODUCTION

"The glory of God is man fully alive; but man's life is the vision of God."[1] During the late '60s, this text was often written on banners which were used in the Mass. Unfortunately, the people who made these banners used only the first part of the quote, thus suggesting that religion is man-centered. The second half of the quote demonstrates that man needs an experience of the knowledge of God which goes beyond his natural powers and requires the grace of revelation to be complete. Irenaeus's phrase "fully alive" expresses this fundamental truth.

This book is offered as a meditation on many different aspects of what it means for man to be "fully alive." Though many of the chapters grew out of talks given on different occasions to different audiences, their common underlying theme is a central topic in Theology. This central theme is the ordering of man in all of his powers, both physical and spiritual, to God.

In Chapter One, I take up what may be the most important and most difficult question in Theology, the basis for the ordering of man to God. Just why is man fully alive when he sees God? What power in the human soul is the source of this supernatural point of view? How is nature ordered to grace?

Once this question is answered, Chapter Two explores the whole man in the thought of Pope John Paul II, with special emphasis on the relation of the body to the supernatural point of view. Pope John Paul has written very eloquently in many places on the fact that the ordering of man to God is not something which concerns the soul only, but can also be applied to the body, as in the sacrament of marriage.

One important application of the supernatural orientation of man is that of human fatherhood. Among the problems of everyday spiritual life, few are more pressing than the question of how the father in the family images

God the Father. Equally important to the understanding of marriage and what the Pope calls the "theology of the body" (how the body participates in the supernatural order) is the idea of spiritual parenting and how one becomes holy in marriage. This is the topic of Chapter Three.

Man realizes this supernatural end by means of his free human choices and so this choice is the topic of the next chapter. Many today question whether there are specific acts that always and everywhere lead to realizing this supernatural destiny or lead away from it. This is the topic of Chapter Four. A key aspect of this question concerns the basic controlling image of this book, which has been variously expressed as form/matter or body/spirit. In the case of the act of free choice, the concept of form/matter becomes crucial.

The body/soul image and its relation to God is the unifying image of the next three chapters. In Chapter Five I explore this image as it affects the right of every human being to life. Here the basic document I use is Evangelium Vitae of Pope John Paul II. Though the teaching of this encyclical is commonly known, I want to mine this teaching and try to get its deep roots in traditional Catholic thought. In Chapters Six and Seven, I take up a much-debated current issue closely related to the problem of life: the problem of death. I first want to treat of modern misunderstandings of death especially as they relate to the body/spirit concept and also as they affect a true understanding of the problem of human destiny. Modern misunderstandings not only alter our understanding of the purpose of our lives, but also our understanding of the purpose and nature of Christ's death. In Chapter Seven, I give the true solution to both difficulties.

The most important means established by Christ to redeem both our souls and our bodies is the sacrament of the Holy Eucharist. Chapter Eight deals with the nature of the Holy Eucharist as the Body of Christ, with special emphasis on how this body redeems us. This mystery encompasses the whole gamut of the relationship of body and soul in the sacraments to nourish man's desire for God.

This book makes use of a lot of terms from Scholastic theology. I would like to define and clarify some of these terms here as they will be used throughout the book. Others I will explain in their proper place.

One basic distinction which will figure heavily in many of the chapters of this book is the distinction between form and matter. This distinction is derived from Aristotelian Physics. Many philosophers in the ancient world tried to explain how things could change and yet remain the same. They thought at first that all change could be explained by material elements, but it proved impossible to explain how things could change and be the same on that basis alone. After several centuries, they discovered that there must be two priniciples which explain the inner composition of every being which changes. One is the subject which receives the change; the other is the change itself. For instance, in the change a sculptor works on a block of marble, the marble is the receiver of the change and the shape of the marble is the character of the change itself. The receiver is the material of the statue and the shape is the form. Hence, ancient philosophers, especially Aristotle, came to affirm that all beings, even natural ones, were composed of matter, the receiver or substratum of any change, and form, the actual nature of the change itself. When this is applied to man, the matter is the body and the reasoning soul is the form. This book explores in depth the question of the matter and form of man, or his body and soul.

It is my hope that this book will help modern Catholics discern just how important the traditional teaching of the Church is to a complete appreciation of man. "Man fully alive," both body and soul, can only be man when he sees God in heaven. The human person arrives at this through his acts of free choice, among them parenting and marriage, so essential to the formation and development of the image of God in man. Death is not the completion of this image, but an experience one must undergo and make sense of in regard to this image. The Eucharist is an especially powerful aid to preparing us for heaven. Only when all of these questions are understood can one see how grace can truly perfect nature and not destroy it.

Chapter 1
THE NATURAL DESIRE TO SEE GOD

The Catholic Church teaches that grace perfects nature. Grace is the completion of the powers of the human soul, and some part of the human soul is naturally *capax Dei* (apt for God). This aptitude for God is affirmed at the very beginning of the Catechism of the Catholic Church: "The desire for God is written in the human heart, because man is created by God and for God; and God never ceases to draw man to himself. Only in God will he find the truth and happiness he never stops searching for: 'The dignity of man rests above all on the fact that he is called to communion with God.'"[2] The Catechism underlines this fact by quoting the famous dictum of St. Augustine, "You have made us for yourself and our heart is restless until it rests in you."[3]

All Catholic theologians agree on this truth. There has been a problem for many years, however, in explaining why this desire exists and how it is fulfilled. What power is this desire found in? How can this desire be said to be natural and yet not lead to a true need for the divine aid of grace? Just how is nature said to desire grace? The solution to this problem can be gleaned from an examination of the implications of a famous Thomistic difficulty which engendered much discussion at the beginning of the 20th century: the problem of the "Natural Desire to See God."

The origin of the difficulty is a famous commentary on the Summa Theologiae of Thomas Aquinas made by Cardinal Thomas de Vio Cajetan (1469-1534). The difficulty is based on a solution Cajetan offered to the problem of human destiny in St. Thomas. Though St. Thomas often speaks of a natural desire to see God,[4] Cardinal Cajetan believed that to posit such a natural desire destroyed the gratuitous character of grace. Instead he formulated a hypothetical state of pure nature to explain how human destiny is completed.

According to Cajetan, when one says that man has a natural capacity for God one must make a distinction in the use of the term "nature". One must first consider nature hypothetically in what is called his "pure nature." This nature merely considers the powers of the human soul, which are observable to anyone, prescinding from any actual historical state of nature. This is nature as Aristotle would have observed it. Aristotle knew and described well the powers of the human soul: intellect, will, emotions, body. If one were to consider the powers of the intellect, will, emotions and body merely as universals abstracting from how they were created in history by God, Cajetan maintained there was no ordering to God in himself. "Nature is not endowed with an inclination to something which the whole power of nature cannot arrive at."[5] If man had been created with this nature, hypothetically he could have been happy to know God only through his effects, as the philosophers do. This would be true even after death.

Cajetan knew that it was defined doctrine that the happiness of man can only consist in the Beatific Vision in which a person knows God face to face, that is to say without the medium of a concept. How then to explain that the Beatific Vision was the destiny or fulfillment of man? Cajetan said that God did not create man in this hypothetical state of pure nature. The historical nature or the human nature which God actually created is different from the hypothetical nature. God created man in the state of grace. This is defined doctrine. It is because of this creation in the state of grace that man is now ordered to heaven or the Beatific Vision as an end.

This theory, called the two-end theory, has powerfully influenced the theology of nature and grace for the last four hundred years. Cajetan's ideas about St. Thomas, and especially about the possibility of the state of pure nature, were considered so authoritative that his commentary was printed at the bottom of the page in the Leonine edition of the critical text of the Summa.

There are many difficulties with this solution- for one, it is philosophically impossible for a being to have a nature with two completely different ends - and even in Cajetan's own day, his commentary was considered problematic. Dominic Soto, a famous contemporary of Cajetan who was an authority at the Council of Trent, wrote, "This commentary destroys the text, it is full of turns and windings."[6]

Nevertheless, most scholars considered the solution of Cajetan normative for many centuries. One example is the famous manual of dogmatic theology by Ludwig Ott, Fundamentals of Catholic Dogma, where the author gives as a "Merely Possible State of Nature" two conditions which he calls the "state of pure nature"(*status purae naturae*) and "unimpaired nature" (*status naturae integrae*). In the first, man can be happy with knowing God only through his effects, his hypothetical or possible natural end, and he is given the preternatural gifts to do this "with ease and certainty."[7]

The problem was that no one could see how the vision of God, which is certainly a supernatural activity, could be the natural end of man without man having the ability to arrive at it. The companion problem was that scholars regarded the term "natural desire" to mean an appetite of the will, which demands knowledge and freedom. The axiom is: *Nihil volitum nisi praecognitum* (Nothing is willed unless it is first foreknown). It is difficult to see how there can be a natural desire for God which is innate and yet a moral appetite at the same time. If it is innate and moral, then God is bound by justice to give grace to fulfill it, which would destroy the freedom of God in giving grace and would make grace due in justice to nature.

There are texts in St. Thomas which do refer to the will desiring God and deny that there is a natural desire for this. One interesting example is:

> When, therefore, by his own reason with the help of divine grace he grasps as his happiness any particular good in which his happiness really does consist, then he merits, not because he desires happiness (which he naturally desires), but because he desires this particular good (which he does not naturally desire) – for example, the vision of God, in which his happiness does in truth consist.[8]

This text addresses the distinction between beatitude which all men desire in any act of the will, and what the particular good is, in which that beatitude consists which all men do not desire. It is primarily about morals, then.

There is another group of negative texts, which refer to the objection: "Something cannot be naturally desired which cannot be attained." St. Thomas often expressed this principle in many ways, using various terms for desire like "inclination" and "potency." In the issue at hand, these all refer to the same power in things.[9] These texts led Cajetan and others to identify the natural desire with a desire of the will and so to say that one could not find any desire (and therefore necessity) for the vision of God in any power of human nature considered in itself.

The Catholic faith does teach that the vision of God in heaven is the only true, objective final happiness of man. Cajetan held that man was not created in the hypothetical state of pure nature, but that his nature was changed and forever altered from what it would have been without grace by the fact that Adam and Eve were created already enjoying the gift of sanctifying grace. Man's creation in grace was, in fact, defined by the Council of Trent and taught by all Catholic theologians.

> The Church, interpreting the symbolism of biblical language in an authentic way, in the light of the New Testament and Tradition,

> teaches that our first parents, Adam and Eve, were constituted in an original 'state of holiness and justice.' This grace of original holiness was 'to share in . . . divine life.[10]

According to Cajetan, this was the reason that human beings now enjoyed a supernatural destiny. Had God not created them with grace, they could have been perfectly happy knowing God only as the cause of the world. There was no human power in itself ordered to something beyond the capabilities which knowledge, by abstraction from sensible experience, could satisfy.

For many centuries this solution was considered normative. The first person to object strongly and forcefully to it was the Jesuit Henri de Lubac. Fr. De Lubac discovered just how contradictory this solution truly was. Though there is the admitted problem of nature having an end which it cannot attain, the solution of Cajetan caused an even worse problem. Any nature with two ends must be two complete and distinct natures. Instead of grace perfecting nature, it seemed at best to replace and at worse to destroy nature.

Fr. de Lubac made the clarification of the problem of human destiny the most important work of his life. He published a book called *Surnaturel*, in which he criticized the traditional solution and offered his own. He was silenced from writing on this question by the Holy See for several years, but later exonerated. After he was exonerated he sought to correct his book, which was later published in two volumes whose English titles are, Augustinianism and Modern Theology[11] and The Mystery of the Supernatural[12].

In the first volume, Fr. de Lubac gives a very effective criticism of the traditional solution of Cajetan, using the Jansenist heresy as a context. De Lubac believes that the two-end solution of Cajetan was the reason the Church had such great difficulty dealing with the Jansenist heresy, which was principally about grace as interpreted by St. Augustine. According to Fr. de Lubac, Jansenism was like

Pelagianism in maintaining that man could persevere in grace by his own power, but differed in that the Jansenists maintained this happened in the state of Original Justice, before the sin of Adam, rather than the state of Original Sin, as the Pelagians argued.

The odd thing is that many people knew Cajetan was incorrect in his interpretation of St. Thomas on many questions. Gilson wrote to Fr. de Lubac to express appreciation for his work and expressed his own experience with the Thomists who followed Cajetan's commentary:

> It seems to me that Cajetan is done for. Very soon we'll be called upon to stand up for him, and I've already started. I'm fully aware that sometimes I overdo it, but after due reflection and in all objectivity, I think I would still label it a *corruptorium*. For two reasons.[sic] His commentary on the first article of the *Summa Theologiae* topples the whole book off the track from the very outset; then, representing himself as interpreting the meaning of the work; he proceeds to lead Saint Thomas' readers astray. It took me years to figure that out. When I finally did, and said something about it, I was afraid it would be a shock to everyone; I was astonished that I got no reaction at all. I did not know everybody already knew this, but wanted to keep the *skeleton in the cupboard!*[13]

In The Mystery of the Supernatural, Fr de Lubac gives his own solution to the question. This is more problematic than his criticism of Cajetan. Cajetan had maintained that nature as a whole, the abstract nature, was changed by the gift of grace in man's original creation. However, Cajetan considered abstract nature to include each individual. De Lubac makes a distinction between abstract nature, which is created by God, and the addition of a supernatural destiny, which is given to each individual. This is further distinguished from the gift of grace, which God gives to fulfill this supernatural destiny.

> If, by a legitimate and necessary process of analysis, we distinguish these three things even more clearly, by staggering, so to say, in time – the fact of the creation of a spiritual being, the supernatural finality imprinted upon that being's nature, and finally the offer presented to his free choice to share in the divine life – we shall have to recognize that the first thing does not necessarily imply the second, nor the second the third, in any sense that would inhibit God's utter independence.[14]

In attempting to ally grace and nature more closely, Fr. de Lubac has created a third element, the supernatural finality placed in nature but different from nature itself. This is like a wedge between nature and grace. "Considered in itself, statistically one might say, my nature or my essence is not more than what it is," De Lubac writes, "there is, let me repeat, no slightest element of the supernatural in it, nor the slightest power to raise itself up to it, nor the smallest principle for laying claim to it."[15] Though this statement is certainly true, the problem of the natural desire does not address this. There is certainly nothing actually supernatural in created nature until one receives grace. The question remains, though, is there a potential to receive grace found in some power of the human soul? Man may not be able to get grace by nature, nor would it be in his nature as created, but should grace be in his nature for him to be able to fulfill <u>all</u> of his powers? Man can certainly have an end without having the necessary means to get there.

This question is never addressed because the supernatural perfection or finality of man is distinguished in De Lubac's solution from "the creation of a spiritual being."

"Thus, it is never nature, which of itself has any call on the supernatural: it is the supernatural which, so to say, must summon up nature before nature can be in a position to receive it."[16]

In distinguishing created nature from the supernatural destiny given to it, de Lubac seems to say that the only reason man must be fulfilled in heaven is because God gave *each individual* this call in creation. This call is not a part of the nature in which all men share, nor of their powers. It is certainly not found in any particular power of the human soul that could have been examined by philosophers like Aristotle. This peculiar distinction between abstract and concrete nature regarding ends seems to be a kind of nominalism, a judgement that universals are not real. Even more strange is the fact that when supernatural destiny is added to the mix as a third element, nature and grace are at once more separated and less distinct than in Cajetan's solution. There seems to be a peculiar metaphysical error at the basis of this solution, which reflects the basic principle of modern philosophy that universals in knowledge, in this case abstract nature, are impoverished experiences of the senses, in this case of the individual man.

The difficulty in resolving this question is compounded by the theologian Karl Rahner, S.J. Rahner wrote on this question many times; and his solution is extremely important because it is here that the famous term "supernatural existential" is explained. In "Concerning the Relationship between Nature and Grace,"[17] Rahner gives a precise summary of his solution: "*This* knowledge is what allows him to distinguish and delimit what he [man] always is (his concrete, indissoluble 'quiddity') into what is this unexacted real receptivity, the supernatural existential, and what is leftover as remainder when this inmost centre is subtracted from the substance of his concrete quiddity, his 'nature'."[18] These two things are then distinguished from the actual experience of grace. As in the work of Fr. de Lubac, here one can see three elements: abstract nature, the supernatural existential, and grace, as opposed to two: nature and grace. One can also see an even deeper distinction between abstract and concrete nature. In fact, for Rahner, if one subtracts the concrete ordering to grace found in individual nature (the supernatural existential) from nature as a universal, one cannot even know what nature really is.

> 'Nature' in the theological sense (as opposed to nature as the substantial content of an entity always to be encountered in contingent fact), i.e. as the concept contraposed to the supernatural, is consequently a remainder concept (*Restbegriff*). . . . Thus there is no way of telling *exactly* how his nature left to itself alone would react, what precisely it would be for itself alone.[19]

One can see here the same nominalism present in Rahner as in de Lubac - only here one cannot even define nature when the ordering to grace, the supernatural existential, is subtracted from it! If one cannot define it, why posit that this nature should exist? The distinction between nature and grace is practically erased. Grace does not perfect nature, it becomes nature. Though Rahner did not want to make these two concepts so distant and at the same time so unified, this is what results from his own poor metaphysics. Though he wanted to affirm absolute truths, his metaphysics does not support the reality of universal ideas. After a long analysis of his philosophy of knowledge, a follower of Rahner's concludes, "[I]t is not transparently clear how conceptual thought in Rahner's own epistemological system can be preserved from relativisation."[20]

The criticism of Fr. de Lubac of the traditional solution of Cajetan is correct and very well argued. But the solutions of both Fr. de Lubac and Fr. Rahner to this problem of the natural desire to see God are both worse than the solutions of Cajetan because they destroy human nature though a peculiar nominalistic Metaphysics. Their intention was to be more explicit about grace fulfilling nature. Instead, they just succeeded in separating them more on the one hand and, strangely, almost making them the same thing on the other, as in the case of Fr. Rahner.

The teaching of St. Thomas is simple and yet has been obscured because of both a voluntarism which reduces the idea of the natural desire to a desire of the will and nominalism which does not recognize universal nature as something real. Both these mistaken solutions present a range of difficulties.

If there is no natural desire to see God, the vision of God cannot be the happiness of man. Happiness or beatitude implies the satisfaction of all desires by perfecting them in act. Satisfaction refers to the fulfillment of the potential present in any composed being for the fitting act which realizes this potential. If there is no power in the soul, which has the knowledge of God in himself as its perfection, then there is no natural potential to be satisfied by knowing God in Himself and therefore God is not the happiness of man. This is against the teaching of the Church.

> The Beatitudes respond to the natural desire of happiness in man. [. . .] The Beatitudes reveal the goal of human existence, the ultimate end of human acts: God calls us to his own beatitude. This vocation is addressed to each individual personally . . . The New Testament uses several expressions to characterize the beatitude to which God calls man: [. . .] – the vision of God.[21]

Man could not be called personally to this happiness if it fulfilled nothing about his person, his rational nature. Also, if there is no natural desire, one cannot explain the punishment of the damned, in whom the natural desire remains even though they can never fulfill it. In them freedom and nature disagree.

If the supernatural order is not needed to fulfill any natural power of the human soul, then grace does not perfect nature. Instead, grace destroys or replaces nature.

Finally, Cajetan's hypothetical state of pure nature would be possible in which human beings would satisfy their powers with only knowing God as cause to effect as is the case with the pagan philosophers. The Thomists have defended this state of pure nature with great gusto, but unfortunately this makes grace a nice afterthought - something good to have, but not essential to nature.

The philosophers can only know God by reason, but this is not a condition of some pure nature, neutral with respect to knowing God. Instead, it is characteristic of fallen nature. Only one who can know God in Himself, by faith here and vision in heaven (theological man), is in the truly natural state. There is no neutral state.

Two companion problems to this doctrine are the concept of limbo and the gratuity of grace. St. Thomas and many other authors maintain that the children in limbo are naturally happy. This does not mean they are fulfilled; it merely means that they never had the opportunity of making personal choices because they had not reached the age of reason when they died. Though they are not ontologically fulfilled in their powers, they do not know what they are missing. They are not worthy of personally experiencing their loss of heaven as a punishment.

As to the gratuity of grace, this is treated in the encyclical of Pius XII, Humani Generis, which states: "Others destroy the true 'gratuity' of the supernatural order, since they think that God cannot produce beings endowed with intellect without ordering and calling them to the beatific vision."[22] This text does not relate to the problem. If, as most interpreters of St. Thomas think, the natural desire refers to an appetite of the will, which would have to involve freedom, then God would have to create an intellectual being with grace already by some sort of justice. If natural desire means an appetite of the will, then morally one must have supernatural consent from the moment of creation, which is impossible without a body developed enough to support rational actions.

In fact, the natural desire does *not* refer to an appetite of the will in St. Thomas and this is one of the keys to the solution of the problem. Everyone took this desire to be an appetite. Some thought it was innate, some did not. They identified this desire with happiness and then discussed how it was possible to fulfill this without destroying the gratuity of grace. To save this, most distinguished the natural desire from the powers of the soul. But such is not the case. All the solutions, traditional and modern, approached the problem in this order: happiness, possibility of attainment, natural desire. In fact, the right approach is just the opposite: the fact of the natural desire, then possibility, then happiness. This important ordering is the foundation for several points that help illumine the solution of St. Thomas.

The first point is that the natural desire is not an act, most certainly not an act of the will. "The natural desire is an inclination: the ordering of potency to its act, to its object, a tendency."[23] Every potency has a natural desire for its act.[24] The stone naturally desires rest on the earth; matter naturally desires form; but neither of these has will.

The natural desire to see God is identical with the *power of the intellect*, which desires to know. It does not presuppose knowledge or consciousness and is thus innate and not acquired. The natural desire is not experienced in addition to the existence of the soul; God did not first create man and then give him as an individual the longing for a supernatural destiny. The fact of a supernatural destiny is due to the power of the intellect. It is the tendency of the intellect to the act, which befits and perfects it. For this reason, it cannot be a desire of the will. *Nihil volitum nisi praecognitum* (Nothing is willed unless first known). The natural desire is a potential to know, not knowledge itself.

This desire to know is nothing other than the natural desire with which Aristotle begins his treatment of Metaphysics. It is identical with the intellect and is not separate or added to the soul as such. Desire here does not mean appetite, but expresses the tendency of every being for its perfection.

> Accordingly, he [Aristotle] says, first, that the desire to know belongs by nature to all men. There are three reasons for this. The first is that each thing naturally desires its own perfection. Hence matter is also said to desire form as any imperfect thing desires its perfection. Therefore, since the intellect, by which man is what he is, considered in itself is all things potentially, and becomes them actually only through knowledge, because the intellect is none of the things that exist before it understands them {...}; so each man naturally desires knowledge just as matter desires form.[25]

St. Thomas examines the problem of the destiny of man in several places, using in each case the term "natural desire" in each case. The language and ideas are identical with those found in the first book of the Metaphysics of Aristotle. The natural desire for knowledge of which Aristotle speaks cannot be perfected or satisfied with anything less than the Vision of God in heaven. There are two places where this problem is clearly answered by St. Thomas at some length: Summa contra Gentiles, III, 25-63 with special emphasis on c. 50 and Summa Theologiae I, 12, 1.

In the Summa contra Gentiles, St. Thomas first examines those truths of faith which are open to reason alone (Books 1-3) and those which demand faith to be known (Book 4). He places the problem of human destiny among the former! Philosophers can and have known the truths about human destiny. In Chapter 25, he proves that every intellectual substance has understanding God as its purpose or final end. He uses the same language as Aristotle to prove this.

> Besides, there is naturally present in all men the desire to know the causes of whatever effects are observed. Hence, because of wondering about things that were seen but whose causes were hidden, men first began to think philosophically; when they found the cause, they were satisfied. But the search did not stop until they reached the first cause, for 'then do we think that we know perfectly, when we know the first cause.' [Aristotle, Metaphysics, I, 3 (983a 25)] Therefore, man naturally desires, as his ultimate end, to know the first cause. But the first cause of all things is God. Therefore, the ultimate end of man is to know God.[26]

Is St. Thomas speaking of the knowledge of God's substance without medium such as one has in heaven or is he speaking of philosophical knowledge, that is, the knowledge of God's existence and his attributes? In Chapters 26-49 he examines all the possible things in which people could find the perfection of their souls and finds them all wanting. Among these are the goods of the body and soul such as virtue. He includes the good of knowledge of God gained by reason and even that gained by faith.

> So, that knowledge of God which, when acquired, leaves no knowledge of a knowable object to be desired is essentially this felicity. But this is not the kind of knowledge about God

> that the philosophers were able to get through demonstrations, because, even when we acquire this knowledge, we still desire to know other things that are not known through this knowledge. Therefore, felicity is not found in such knowledge of God.[27]
>
> Moreover, through felicity, because it is the ultimate end, natural desire comes to rest. Now, the knowledge of faith does not bring rest to desire but sets it aflame, since every man desires to see what he believes. So man's ultimate felicity does not lie in the knowledge of faith.[28]

St. Thomas demonstrates that the destiny of human life cannot be in this life because the intellect demands direct knowledge of the first cause. If our destiny were here, then the natural desire would be in vain. As the end must be in the next life, our destiny is the same as the angels'. We have souls without bodies until the general resurrection; the angels are spirits with no bodies. Both of us have intellects. St. Thomas concludes the whole discussion by asking if the natural desire of even the angels can be satisfied with knowing God as their cause. Our souls are substances separated from matter for a time and the angels are spirits separated from matter by nature. The satisfaction of both is the same. There is no state of pure nature mentioned here because the angels do not have a common nature. Each one is unique. Also, since the desire of the intellect refers merely to this power of the soul as such, there is no mention of the grace necessary to attain this desire.

Just as men entered the world of matter and wondered about the causes of the world, the angels contemplate themselves and wonder about their cause. If the intelligence of the angels could be satisfied with knowing God as the cause, *a fortiori* so should that of men.

In Chapter 50, St. Thomas gives no fewer than six arguments, all taken from philosophy, to show that there is a natural desire in the angels (and *a fortiori* in men) to see God. Further, though the intellect of the angels can be perfected in nothing less than the vision of God, this is not because the angels are created in grace. It is the other way around. Since the angels in their very being have the vision of God as their end, a supernatural activity, they must have a supernatural aid to attain this. I will summarize these arguments in the form of six syllogisms (the Latin text is found in the notes).

1. What is imperfect desires its perfection.
   The knowledge the angels have through their own substance is imperfect.
   Therefore, the angels naturally desire to know God in himself and not through his effects.[29]

2. One who knows an effect desires to know its cause.
   The angels know they are effects of God.
   Therefore the angels naturally desire to know the cause in itself.[30]

3. One who knows the existence of something desires naturally to know its essence.
   The angels know that God exists.
   Therefore they naturally desire to know his essence.[31]

4. Nothing finite fulfills the power of the intellect to know.
   The knowledge the angels have of God through their substance is finite.

Therefore the angels cannot fulfill the natural desire of the intellect to know by knowing God through themselves.[32]

5. One who desires knowledge, also desires to flee ignorance.
   The angels know the God surpasses their natural knowledge and so they are ignorant of him.
   Therefore, the angels naturally desire to rid themselves of the ignorance they have in regards to God by knowing his essence.[33]

6. The closer a thing is to the end, the more it desires the end.
   The angels are closer to God in being than man.

Therefore, the angels desire to know God more in his essence than men do.[34]

St. Thomas makes no reference to a state of pure nature or to the fact of man's creation in grace as the basis for the desire for the vision of God in all intellectual substances. The majors of each of the six arguments are drawn from common Metaphysical principles accessible to reason and certainly known by Aristotle.

St. Thomas then draws the evident conclusion from these six arguments: All other human desires and powers can be satisfied with something here on earth, but not this power. The intellect can only be satisfied with knowing God as he is in himself. Man cannot do this here on earth. This can only occur in heaven with the addition of a supernatural light to the human intellect. St. Thomas sums it up graphically: **"Let those men be ashamed then who seek human happiness in lower things when it is so highly situated".**[35]

The question logically arises: If the majors which prove that there is a natural desire to see God were known by Aristotle, why didn't Aristotle speak of seeing God as the end of man? It is well known that Aristotle at the end of his Ethics argues that man can only attain a limited happiness here. St. Thomas himself talks of imperfect happiness. The answer is this: Aristotle knew of no means which made it possible to arrive at such an end. He was too good a scientist to speak about the possibility of attaining something for which no means existed. The man known to Aristotle was like the fox before the grapes. The grapes were delicious, but unreachable, so the fox went away sad.[36] Aristotle did not know that the man he knew by his ordinary experience was not man as he should be, but fallen man. He did not know about the Scriptures. To talk of arriving at a final end for which there was no means, in this case sanctifying grace, would have been nonsense to him.

After St. Thomas proves the existence of the natural desire to see God, he then goes on to ask how it is possible to attain it. This demands grace and can only be fulfilled in heaven. St. Thomas then concludes that this fulfillment is the happiness of man.

The same doctrine is contained in Summa Theologiae, I, 12, 1. Here, too, the argument is metaphysical. The question concerns the possibility of knowing God in his essence. St. Thomas states that to maintain one could never know God in his essence is not only against faith, but also *against reason*! The reason is that as he maintained in the Summa contra Gentiles, "there is a natural desire in man for knowing the cause of something when he considers an effect. From this wonder arose in men. If therefore the intellect of the reasoning creature could not reach the first cause of things, the natural desire of nature will remain in vain. Thus it must simply be granted that the blessed see the essence of God."[37]

Once the natural desire has been identified with the power of the intellect to know the ultimate truth, then the possibility of attaining it must be after this life. A special light over and above the lights of reason and faith is necessary, the light of glory. (SCG, cc. 51-62). Finally, St. Thomas determines this vision of God received through the light of glory to be the happiness of man.(SCG, c. 63). The will seeks the perfection of all human powers. The highest human power is the power of the intellect. Only the experience of the vision of God can bring the intellect to perfection, and therefore only the vision of God can truly make man happy and be the goal of man's moral actions.

Both from reason and faith, then, one must concur that the very nature of man is fulfilled only in the vision of God. This end must be the basis for all human choices. Here the question of the will and the means enter, but presupposing *the already determined end*. "Although man is inclined to an ultimate end by nature, yet he cannot attain that end by nature, but only by grace because of the exalted character of the end."[38]

But what of the point that positing a supernatural end to a power of nature seems to compromise the gratuity of grace? Does not Aristotle say that there must be a natural agent that corresponds to every natural inclination? For a potential to be truly natural, must not the natural agent have the ability to realize it by nature?

It is true that for every natural potential there must be a natural agent, but this agent need not actively realize the potential by its own power. This agent can only dispose for the reception of the action.

> It does not make any difference, regarding this question, if the active principle answers to the passive principle in nature with respect to the ultimate perfection, namely of form; or with respect to the disposition which is necessary for the ultimate form, as is the case in the generation of man according to the position of

> the faith, or even in all other things according to the opinion of Plato and Avicenna.[39]

In the case of man, faith teaches that the parents prepare the matter as the dispositive material cause, but God creates the soul. The parents have a natural potency, but it is a dispositive receptive potential. They do not have the active power in themselves to create the soul; that demands a direct action on the part of God.

In the case of grace, man allows himself to be justified by grace by the disposition of his consenting will to the action of God. Of course, God's aid is still necessary here through actual grace to move him to consent. This is despite the fact that only God produces justification in us. Yet God never justifies a man against his will. He never induces a supernatural effect if the dispositions of the nature he has created are not properly prepared to receive that effect. In this case, that disposition is human freedom.

> Therefore, that effect, which is produced without medium only by God, and yet there is in the recipient a natural order for receiving that effect in no other way than through God will not be a miracle. This is clear in the infusion of the reasoning soul and also in the justification of sinners; because there is a natural order in the soul for the righteousness leading to justification.[40]

The disposition spoken of here is the consent to be justified. This is a positive openness to receive which man has in his nature by his will, just as he has in his nature the positive need for God to fulfill the intellect by vision.[41] The whole of human life consists in preparation for grace, which God will give because he has infallibly promised he will.

Grace, then, perfects nature because of the presence of the intellect in man. God could not create a human nature which would be neutral regarding the perfective necessity of grace, because such a being would lack an intellect and would thus not be human. But arriving at that end is something for which there is no natural power in man. Man has only a natural, receptive and passive potential by which he can prepare himself to receive God's grace - the only possible means by which he could realize this destiny. The fact that the vision of God is man's destiny is due to the intellect. The actual attainment of that destiny is due to the will filled with the supernatural gift of divine grace. Unless he attains the fulfillment of this natural desire through a supernatural appetite, man will never be perfectly happy.

> Unhappy is the one who does not know you, even if he knows all the other things (created things). Happy is the one who knows you even if he knows nothing else. The one who knows you and all the other things is not any happier for knowing all the other things than for knowing you alone.[42]

Chapter 2
THE PERSON IN THE THEOLOGY OF THE BODY OF POPE JOHN PAUL II

"Man stands in the middle of creation, on the horizon of being, between flesh and spirit, between time and eternity."[43] This quote is suggested by a text from The Book of Causes, written by the early neo-Platonist philosopher Proclus, and is quoted many times by Scholastic theologians, including St. Albert the Great and St. Thomas Aquinas. It perfectly expresses the fact that the human person is a spiritual being. It also demonstrates that the body is an essential component of the human person. Following on the determination of man's destiny, the next logical question is the relation of the supernatural order to man composed of body and soul. His destiny must relate to both aspects of his being: the spiritual and the material. These must not be divorced from each other in man's relationship with God.

Throughout history many heresies have divorced the body from the soul, not least the Albigensian heresy which St. Dominic founded the Dominican Order to combat. The Albigensians believed that all matter was evil. They practiced abortion and considered the spiritual order to be completely divorced from the physical. Matter and spirit could have no true relation to each other.

There are modern variations on the theme of this divorce. The first and greatest of its proponents is usually considered to be Descartes, who maintained that no knowledge was certain which came from the senses. He therefore tried to bypass the senses in discovering the certainty of human knowledge. It is to Descartes that we owe the idea of the soul in the body as the "ghost in the machine," in which soul and body have no necessary relation to each other.

The Eighteenth-century philosopher Immanuel Kant divided matter and spirit still further by denying that sense experience has any place in truly reasonable knowledge. For

Kant, the person casts a web of intelligibility around known objects in such a way that there is no relation between knowledge and the thing known which the subject does not supply. Objective truth becomes subjective. Knowledge through the senses cannot lead to metaphysical truth, but is limited to what can be described or the empirical. This is true not only of theoretical truths, but also of universal ideas like moral laws.

Kant denies that morals have anything to do with perfecting the powers of the person. Instead, he finds the source of ethical obligation in an *a priori* categorical imperative that has no relation to any of the powers of the soul. Freedom of will, for him, has no relation to the knowledge gained by sense experience; the mind casts a web of intelligence, and desire casts a web of good, around things in the world which they do not possess in themselves. In Kant, thus, there is a complete "rupture"[44] between the subject and the object. Something is only universally true or good as it fulfills one's personal needs.

> The categories do not, even by means of pure intuition, afford us any cognition of things; they can only do so in so far as they can be applied to empirical intuition.
>
> Space and time, as conditions of the possibility of the presentation of objects to us, are valid no further than for objects of sense, consequently, only for experience. Beyond these limits they represent to us nothing, for they belong only to sense, and have no reality apart from it.[45]

The Pope summarizes Kant in two points.

> [Kant] 1) has taken away the essence itself of the ethical life of the sphere of the empirical

> experience of the person and has transferred it to the extraempirical, noumenous sphere; 2) has crystallized the entire ethical experience of the personal subject in only one and unique psychological element, that is to say in the sentiment of respect for the law.[46]

This "rupture" between subject and object leads to consideration of truth in morals, in which there really is no philosophy of the place for the body or emotions or anything else based on sense experience. For Kant, morality is based on absolutely fixed laws, much like physical laws, which are not based on conclusions of the senses, but are undefined postulates of every desire. This leads to considerable difficulties. An ethics of sexuality, for example, cannot be developed from an examination of the manner in which human beings carry on personal relations with each other in the sexual sphere. It drops from an *a priori* cloud that cannot be scrutinized with man's ordinary sense knowledge.

Descartes and Kant have their powerful representatives in modern Catholic theology, perhaps most evidently in moral theology. Speaking of such misunderstandings of the human act, in Veritatis Splendor, Pope John Paul II wrote, "*A doctrine which dissociates the moral act from the bodily dimensions of its exercise is contrary to the teaching of Scripture and Tradition.* Such doctrine revives, in new forms, certain ancient errors which have always been opposed by the Church, inasmuch as they reduce the human person to a 'spiritual' and purely formal freedom."[47]

One cannot wonder that Pope John Paul II has sought to clarify the exact nature of the relation of body to soul. Moreover, his teaching has broad applications to other difficulties in the present teaching of the Church, and it also perfectly reflects St. Thomas' philosophical and theological conclusions regarding the relations among the body, soul, and moral freedom. The Pope's clarification of this relationship has much to do with his ideas about the human person.

The foundation of the Pope's explanation is what he calls the "theology of the body", a term that expresses his ideas about the unity of the body and the soul in the human person. "In fact, *body and soul are inseparable*: in the person, in the willing agent and in the deliberate act *they stand or fall together*."[48] The Pontiff makes clear that the "theology of the body" is based on a "total vision of man"[49] which must "be constructed from the 'beginning'".[50] This beginning refers to the time before the original sin described in the book of Genesis; it has traditionally been called the "state of original justice or integrity."

In this original happy state of inner integrity, Adam is asked to name the animals. (Gen. 2:19-20) He does this on the basis of sense experience but also as the result of infused knowledge. In the process he discovers no animal which is like himself - so man experiences "original solitude". As a sign of his difference from the animals, man is given self-knowledge and self-determination. These are rooted in qualities traditionally termed the intellect and will, and they cause man to be a partner in realizing his own destiny. They are the expression of human subjectivity.

But it is not only the intellect and will which express the subjectivity of man; the body expresses it also. "Man is a subject not only because of his self-awareness and self-determination, but also on the basis of his own body. The structure of the body is such as to permit him to be the author of truly human activity. In this activity the body expresses the person." [51]

The Pope points out that the body is the expression of the personal subject who is man. The spiritual nature of man that sets him apart from the animals originates in his soul. But his body expresses this difference also, because man is a composite of two complementary principles: a reasoning soul and a material body. This union of the soul with the body is so deep that no bodily act that includes freedom can be judged by the body's standards alone. Though the body and the soul are two distinct principles, they command a marvelous union in acting. This is true of every truly human act, but especially true in the act of sexuality.[52] The sexual act cannot be reduced merely to the body, nor can any moral evaluation of the sexual act treat the body as a mere "cadaver" in the human person. By a "cadaver" here I mean that the actions done in the body are never ethically neutral, cannot be considered to have no implications for the perfection of the person, and therefore cannot be performed with impunity or with no consequences beyond the merely physical. The human person is a unity of body and soul.

Because of this unity, the purpose and use of the sexual act always have personal consequences. This is true for the parties to the act who have souls and express their union of soul by means of this act. It is true for the child, who has a soul and is born as a result of this act. Finally, it is true for God, who created this act to let created beings experience the personal communion and creating life of the Trinity and thus to be in his image and to bring forth little trinities, children made in his image and likeness.

In his expression of unity, John Paul II invokes the celebrated philosophical idea of the relation of the soul to the body described by Aristotle and the Scholastics and invoked in Vatican II, which stated that "the rational soul is *per se et essentialiter* the form of the body. The spiritual and immortal soul is the principle of unity of the human being, whereby it exists as a whole - *corpore et anima unus* - as a person."[53] The Catechism of the Catholic Church teaches the same doctrine using the same philosophical tradition: "The unity of soul and body is so profound that one has to consider the soul to be the 'form' of the body: i.e., it is because of its spiritual soul that the body made up of matter becomes a living, human body; spirit and matter, in man, are not two natures united, but rather their union forms a single nature."[54]

Pope John Paul discussed this problem in several articles he wrote as a philosophy professor but which, sadly, have not yet been published in English. In these works, he analyzes the ideas of modern philosophy, especially those of Immanuel Kant and Max Scheler, and applies them to the ideas of St. Thomas and Aristotle on the nature of moral and personal acts. In the pages that follow, I will examine some passages translated from the Italian editions of these works to help illuminate a proper solution to the problem of the body and the soul. The Pope points out that in the area of morals we most clearly perceive the implications of erroneous notions of the relation of body to soul. Again, two of the authors who have caused an erroneous idea of this relationship are Descartes and Kant.

According to Pope John Paul, the great difficulty this relationship poses for modern philosophy is first perceived in Descartes. As is well known, Descartes was fascinated, and a little intimidated, by the problem of certainty in knowledge. His difficulties led him to doubt all knowledge gained from the senses as certain and have reference only to his own internal reason. As a result, Descartes denied that body and soul have any intrinsic relationship at all. "The division of man into external substance, that is the body, and thinking substance, that is the soul, was characteristic of Descartes. The two remain in a parallel relationship and do not create one whole, one substantial *compositum humanum*."[55]

The divorce of the experience of the senses from the knowledge of truth is also felt in the realm of morals. The principle representative of this divorce is Immanuel Kant, who has had a great influence on modern philosophy. The ideas of Kant on the contribution of sense experience to both truth in itself and the truth of morals have immense implications for the understanding of the person. Kant held that nothing in itself was understandable or true. The truth of the world and of morals had to shift from the object to the subject. He did not think that one could discover the truth of either from an examination of the world through the senses. Rather, one found within himself a "categorical imperative" which demanded both the metaphysical and moral truth. Knowledge gained through the senses was not possible and so the criteria for determining the truth of knowledge were shifted in all cases from the object to the inner needs of the subject.

By contrast, John Paul II states that the tradition of the Church, expressed by Aristotle and St. Thomas, makes clear that the person is the efficient cause of his own acts and therefore of his own perfection in morals. Moral perfection means that one realizes all the potentials which are present in the powers of his soul. The perfection of knowledge, for example, is truth. The perfection of the emotions is to feel in accordance with reason. The perfection of the will is the good of all the powers of man according to the truth of reason, his highest faculty.

"I therefore live myself, my own person, as efficient cause of the good and evil of my own person."[56] The person who is the efficient cause of his own perfection attains this perfection using acts which express his substantial union of body and soul. For that reason, the will seeks perfection which is given a specific character by all the powers of the soul in their relation to human perfection.

> It is for this that St. Thomas, following the conception of Aristotle, leaves somewhat apart all the other empirical coefficients of experience and occupies himself above all with its essential character, namely in the actualization of the will connected either with the action of practical reason or with the action of emotional factors, and finally with all the other factors which, thanks to the their belonging to the *compositum humanum* (human composite), participate in the ethical act.[57]

One great reaction to the rupture Kant proposed between the subject and the object occurred at the end of the Nineteenth Century. This was the reaction of Phenomenology, particularly in the thought of Max Scheler. John Paul II states that Scheler rightly reacted against Kant's over-intellectualizing in morals, which rejected any participation of the order of the senses in the moral judgment. Scheler rightly sought to recover the experience of the senses in moral knowledge. But then Scheler reduced all moral experience to the senses. "When Scheler finds himself face to face with this empirical whole constitutive of the ethical experience of man, he affirms immediately that this experience has the character of the act of the person."[58] He called this "value".[59] In other words, the whole of man's personal experience is reduced to the order of the senses which does not constitute any object for the will.[60] There is no such thing as a moral will in the works of Scheler. The will is reduced to the feelings, which take the place of moral values of the person. "Scheler has founded the entire ethical experience on its secondary elements, because he has deprived it of the backbone of the will."[61]

Thus, the two pillars of the modern philosophy of morals suffer from the divorce of the order of the senses from the order of reason. In Kant, reason is emphasized at the expense of the senses and emotions; in Scheler, raw sense experience (especially of the emotions) is emphasized at the expense of reason and will.

> We affirm therefore that in both conceptions, that of Kant and that of Scheler, so important for the history of philosophy, together with the separation of the old concept of the ethical act have involved a certain deformation of the ethical experience itself.[62]

In another article, Thomistic Personalism,[63] the Pope makes clear that the Thomistic concept of the person is the proper ontological foundation of all phenomenological investigations of the person. But what forms the foundation of the experience of the person in morals, and therefore of those acts which are most characteristic of him? The foundation is the rationality of the person. Indeed, the traditional definition of the person remains the only true one: "The person is an individual substance of rational nature."[64] The ontological foundation of the experience of the person includes all of the powers of the human soul which are traditionally understood as constitutive or connected to the act of free moral choice: i.e. intellect, will and emotions. Hylomorphism, the Aristotelian teaching that matter and form (and in man's case body and soul) form two necessary principles of each created being, is the only correct way to understand the fullness of the foundation in being of the person. Man is made up of the reasoning soul as form and the body as matter.

Though phenomenology can contribute to the study of the person in the psychological sense, this must be founded on the study of the person in the metaphysical sense. Because the human person is a spiritual soul that exists in substantial union with a physical body, the psychological experience of the acting person must include all of the powers of intellect, will and emotions expressed in the free acts that command the body. Descartes, Kant and Scheler separate moral experience from the totality of human experience and emphasize only one facet of it; St. Thomas alone does full justice to the necessary union of all the faculties of man, including his physical faculties in the moral act.

> The faculties in which the spirituality of soul is expressed and actualized, and therefore the spirituality of man are reason and free will. These constitute in a certain sense, the principal means for the realization of the human person; on the grounds of these actions

> the entire psychological and moral personality is modeled. However, these faculties are not the only ones of the human soul because this is the form of the body. [...] St. Thomas perfectly renders an account of them and characterizes the spirituality of man according to reality. In his conception, this one spirituality is such that to it in highest measure the substantial unity is conformed with bodiliness and therefore with sensuality. This union must therefore have a particular role in the formation of the personality of man.[65]

Although modern philosophy makes a valuable contribution in emphasizing the lived experience of individuals, the philosophy of St. Thomas is the key to understanding the composite nature of the human person. The Pope concludes, "Thus in St. Thomas we see very well the person in his objective existence and action, but it is difficult to perceive the lived experience of the person."[66] The lived experience of the person demands first an authentic metaphysics in St. Thomas. Then one can go on to discuss, in the manner of modern phenomenology, the character of that lived experience. But the metaphysical basis of the will and intellect must always be found in the sense experience and ordered to it. Here is where the ideas of the Pope differ very much from those of Scheler. The Pope's personalism can be summed up, "Man represents a *compositum* which is spiritual-material, rational-sensitive, thus the energies of sensual love also act in him, but in any case his love is properly spiritual love."[67]

The Pope's teaching on the nature of the person can be applied in many areas. One application he himself makes is to sexuality, an example in which the lived experience of the person must include a marvelous union of both the spirit and the senses. In <u>Love and Responsibility</u>, where the Pope beautifully summarizes his ideas about marriage, he expresses this lived experience judged by what he calls the "personalistic norm".

> This norm, in its negative aspect, states that the person is the kind of good which does not admit of use and cannot be treated as an object of use and as such the means to an end. In its positive form the personalistic norm confirms this: the person is a good towards which the only proper attitude is love. This positive content of the personalistic norm is precisely what the commandment to love teaches.[68]

In the "original nakedness" –the state of Adam and Eve, naked but not ashamed in the garden (Gen. 2:25) - one returns to the "theology of the body", one of the principal applications of the Pope's notion of Thomistic personalism. The fact that Adam and Eve experienced their similarity in nature and yet difference in sex allowed them to complete the image of the Trinity in their creation. This completion is expressed ethically in the disinterested union of marriage, a union expressed first in our first parents' pure hearts united to God by grace, and expressed in their wills for communion, but ratified in their experience of this union by viewing each other's bodies. "When the first man exclaims, at the sight of the woman, 'This is bone of my bones, and flesh of my flesh," (Gn. 2:23), he merely affirms the human identity of both. Exclaiming in this way, he seems to say: here is *a body that expresses the "person!"*[69]

What man does in the body has immense ramifications for what is expressed in the soul. Communion of persons is expressed in a lack of shame based on such self-restraining love that expresses the "interior freedom"[70] of man. Since the divine Trinity involves no use or abuse of one another in their persons, man must complete this image in his own proper communion of persons, a communion which takes place in the freedom of both reason and will, <u>and</u> which is expressed in the freedom to make a gift of one's body to another in the sexual realm. This reciprocal freedom both expresses and founds the communion of persons which makes marriage a natural sacrament. "The 'affirmation of the person' is nothing but acceptance of the gift, which, by means of reciprocity, creates the communion of persons. The latter is constructed from within, comprising also the whole 'exteriority' of man, that is everything that constitutes the pure and simple nakedness of the body in its masculinity and femininity."[71]

However, the ability and availability to give oneself and to receive the other in freedom can only be completely experienced if caused by the interior integrity of grace. Since this personhood has God as the example, only union with God can totally cause a whole giving, both interior and exterior. Grace, then, is the cause of the fulfillment of the person and the source of personal, ethical freedom. "If, as we have already said, creation is a gift to man, then his fullness and deepest dimension is determined by grace."[72]

The Pope calls this moral dimension of sexuality the "nuptial meaning of the body". It must be at the foundation of all marital ethics in whatever state of nature the person is found, even the option of persons in the New Testament who offer their virginity in freedom to God, or the choice of individuals in our own day to renounce marriage by embracing virginity and celibacy.

Experience shows that the state of original justice is not easily maintained, and its loss is accompanied by a host of unfortunate consequences. After man sinned, those who were without shame at the presence of each other's bodies acquired shame. But there is no difference in the body-soul composite before and after the sin. What has changed is the relation of the soul to God by grace. The body now becomes the place where such a lack of relationship with God causes an unnatural use, one of extortion and manipulation. Sin is the primordial denial of the personalistic norm. "Only the nakedness that makes woman an 'object' for man, or vice versa, is a source of shame. The fact that 'they were naked and not ashamed' means that the woman was not an 'object' for man nor he for her."[73]

The body in the hylomorphic composite which forms the nature of the human person becomes on the one hand a "sacrament" in which the life of grace is morally expressed in the sexual order, and on the other hand the place where lack of communion with God is also experienced in a graphic and obvious way. "The sacrament, as a visible sign, is constituted with man, as a 'body', by means of his 'visible' masculinity and femininity. The body, in fact, and it alone, is capable of making visible what is invisible: the spiritual and the divine. It was created to transfer into the visible reality of the world the mystery hidden since time immemorial in God, and thus be a sign of it."[74]

The fact that the body is a sign of the invisible returns us to the body/soul composite. This ability of the body to make the soul "visible" avoids the radical dualism of Descartes, the anti-sensual character of Kant's categorical imperative, and the exaggerated sensuality of Scheler's value. Moreover, as the body is a sign of God, and God shows his goodness by disinterestedly bringing forth life, the image of God expressed here is completed in procreation. "In this way a great creative perspective is opened: precisely the perspective of man's existence, which is continually renewed by means of 'procreation' (we could say 'self-reproduction')".[75]

In summary, Pope John Paul II bases his doctrine of the person on St. Thomas's philosophy of being which describes a person as the "most perfect being" (*perfectissimum ens*)[76] in nature. This traditional view reveals the extreme deficiencies of modern philosophy's attempt to deal with the nature of the person. These deficiencies include not only those of Descartes and Kant, who radically divorced the supersensible experience of human reason from the sensible, but also those of Scheler and the phenomenologists, who are unclear about this supersensible or intellectual character. The Pope lauds the efforts of phenomenologists to reintroduce the senses to knowledge and moral life, but argues that they cannot escape the difficulties of older modern philosophers when they fail to do justice to the "human composite" in their philosophy of the person.

Thomas Aquinas and Aristotle alone do justice to the ontological basis for the nature and acts of the person, which include a marvelous union of man's intellect, will and emotions. This union is expressed in actions integrally involved in personal or moral activities, especially those which express moral union, like sexual marital relations. Modern phenomenology can contribute further implications as to how this ontological foundation relates to the daily psychological experience of persons, but this is not a deficiency in St. Thomas, who was simply uninterested in expressing all the implications of this thought for man's daily sensual experience. The "theology of the body", especially as described in Scripture, provides the needed expression of the true lived experience of the union of matter and spirit in the "horizon of being" which is man and man's awareness of himself. This must remain the basic standard by which man's acts are judged. The "theology of the body" is an important expression of "man fully alive".

Brian Mullady, O.P.

Chapter 3
THE FATHERHOOD OF GOD AND THE FATHERHOOD OF MAN IN AN EGALITARIAN AGE

"I believe in God, the Father Almighty, Creator of heaven and earth..." This is the first and most important article of the creed, the one from which all the rest flow. Closely connected to it is the first petition in the greatest of all Christian prayers: "Our Father, who art in heaven, hallowed be thy name." In the relationship of spiritual to physical parenting, we find an excellent application of the "theology of the body" – but this relationship often seems compromised in our Western culture, especially in the character of the father. Because true spiritual fatherhood is essential for the development of "man fully alive", I want to examine the modern problem of fatherhood to demonstrate how man is made in the image of God in all his powers and, I hope, to provide a practical basis for the renewal of fatherhood in the new millennium.

We live in an age of equality, an egalitarian age. Democracy is the watchword for everything worthwhile. In ancient times, democracy was a system of government in which all the people ruled. Most times eras are characterized by basic ideas which, though valid in their own frame of reference, tend to take on a life of their own and morph into metaphysical systems. Bishop Sheen used to call this the "lyricism of culture". Thus, in our times, democracy has come to mean much more than a system of government. Now it means a system of being, truth, metaphysics, even spirituality in which everything is absolutely equal in value and there is no hierarchy of being.

Since the 1960's, this new cultural lyricism has had a great effect on the interpretation of all authority: in the state, in the Church and even in the Godhead. For example, the term "collegiality" is used like a magical incantation to justify the adaptation of all administrative forms to a democratic form. Though Vatican II uses this term to express the communion enjoyed among the bishops among themselves, Pope Paul VI added a note to the document Lumen Gentium to explain in no uncertain terms that this did not mean the bishops were a parliament in which all were equal: "The word *College* is not taken in the *strictly juridical* sense, that is as a group of equals who transfer their powers to their chairman, but as a permanently fixed body whose form and authority is to be ascertained from revelation."[77]

Though this term was not taken to refer to a democracy and was only used to refer to the bishops, many continue to use it to call for democratic authority in all forms of Church societies, especially religious life. This takes the form of "group government" and so-called "open chapters" in religious life in which everyone is involved in decision-making. What actually happens is a subtle (and at times not-so-subtle) form of group manipulation, in which well-meaning religious who have been used to doing what they are told find their lives dominated by political modes of group control learned in psychological T-groups, modes characteristic of the secular state. This smacks of democracy run amuck.

Many years ago C.S. Lewis, the Anglican philosopher of culture and religion, wrote a wonderful essay called "Screwtape Proposes a Toast": a fanciful speech given at a banquet in Hell in which the devil laments that there are no really evil people in the modern world. This is because everyone has adopted mediocrity as a standard - even mediocre evil. Yet though there are no crackingly good villains anymore, Hell is more populated than ever because people do not seek excellence any more and so they are easily led down the path of least resistance. Their very mediocrity keeps them from good.

> *Democracy* is the word with which you must lead them by the nose. The good work which our philological experts have already done in the corruption of human language makes it unnecessary to warn you that they should never be allowed to give this word a clear and definable meaning. [...] But the real end is the destruction of individuals.[78]

The modern destruction of the individual influenced almost every cultural institution. One of the most tragic influences, though, has been on the idea of fatherhood in our culture and religion. The more extreme expressions of this destruction deny all male images to God and seek to remove men from the lives of women and of the family as much as possible.

On the secular front, a new book by David Blankenhorn, Fatherless America, speaks to the problem of the lack of fatherhood and the loss of true masculine identity in our society. According to Blankenhorn, the current crisis in American culture is characterized by the almost complete absence of the father in the family. In fact, there are many who agree. "Today's expert story of fatherhood largely assumes that fatherhood is superfluous."[79]

Since grace builds on nature and perfects it, those who have given up the idea of fatherhood as superfluous to the family consider it superfluous in religious categories. In some cases, fatherhood is seen as not only superfluous but dangerous. This notion is then applied to every figure of authority, whether the superior in religious life, the bishop in the diocese, the pope (a title which comes from an affectionate root of father, "papa") and even God. All forms of patriarchy are to be rejected as the roots of abuse in a culture which views democracy not just as a system of government, but as a metaphysical norm. For example, Rosemary Radford Reuther said in a talk given at the WomanChurch conference in 1983:

> We are WomanChurch, not in exile, but in exodus. We flee the thundering armies of Pharaoh. We are not waiting for a call to return to the land of slavery and to serve as altar girls in the temples of patriarchy. Our brother Jesus did not come to this earth to manufacture this idol and he is not represented by this idol. We cry out –horror, blasphemy, deceit, foul deed. We call on our brothers [here she named some Bishops who were in the audience] to flee with us from this idol with flashing eyes and smoking nostrils who is about to consume the earth. [...] Together let us break up this great idol and grind it into powder, dismantle the great leviathan of violence and misery [...] and transform it back into the means of peace and plenty, so that all children of the earth can sit together at the banquet of life.[80]

During the year of preparation for the beginning of the new Millennium, Pope John Paul II asked us to celebrate the Fatherhood of God. The current crisis calls for us to re-examine what is meant by male images of God and then to try to resuscitate the idea of human fatherhood found in the family against this current of cultural and religious destruction.

Though Jesus uses the name "Father" in many places in the New Testament, the masculine images and names used for God in general are also found in the Old Testament. "I am a father to Israel, and Ephraim is my firstborn" (Jer. 31:9;) "He shall cry to me, 'You are my father, my God and the Rock of my salvation'". (Ps. 89:20) The Father image is, of course, an analogous name, like all names referring to God. An analogous name refers to something which is not so completely different from the thing to which it is being compared as to be completely inexpressive of it, nor so like the thing as to give complete understanding. The term "father" with respect to God is taken from human relationships, which are created. It cannot be applied to God without some change in meaning to befit an infinite being.

For example, as an analogous name, the term "Father" obviously does not denote sex in God, since God has no body. Still, this term does denote certain characteristics of the human male in human relationships, and thus it offers some insight into the characteristics of God when changed to apply to an infinite being. According to the Old Testament, these are power which is supreme coupled with a benevolence which is infinite. This supreme power and infinite benevolence mean that God is wholly other and also without origin. He is therefore not a creature or a part of creation. Heaven is the absolute symbol of God because heaven coupled with power and benevolence represents a transcendent being.

The masculinity of God expresses the fact that He is the only being in whom essence and existence are one. He is above all material creation. Yet this is not the whole picture. If God were only transcendent, if He were only other, He could not relate to his creatures. Many New Age thinkers, following a kind of neo-paganism, have denied the masculine images and pronouns to God in order to make him intimate to us. Certainly, God must be immanent to us; one can approve the purpose of this denial without approving the denial itself. God is immanent to the world, and in all pagan religions the maternal images used for God emphasize that immanence. As the sky or heaven is an image that expresses the transcendence of God, the earth becomes the "Mother", an image that expresses originated life and is an image for His Immanence.

One need only think of the Native American prayer to the Four Directions as opposed to the Three persons of the Trinity. This prayer ends with the invocation addressed to the earth:

We greet you, Great Spirit of the Earth.
It was from you we came as from a Mother;
You nourish us still and give us shelter.

Teach us to walk softly on your lands,
To seek with care your gifts,
To love with tenderness all our brothers and sisters
Who have been born of your goodness.

And when the day comes that you call us back to yourself,
Help us to return to you as a friend,
To find ourselves embraced, encircled, enfolded in your arms.

In this little prayer, the earth is looked on as a womb, like the maternal womb from which man springs forth and to which he returns. Pagan religions place God both in the heavens and in the earth. Not so the Old and New Testament. God is only in the heaven, which represents the life-giving origin of the Father. Jesus prays, "Our Father, who art in heaven," not "Our Father and Mother" or "Our Mother".

It is true that there are times when both the Old Testament and Our Lord use maternal expressions concerning God. By this they wish to emphasize precisely the immanence of God. But though God is intimately present to his creation, he is not a part of it. St. Thomas Aquinas says: "God is in all things, but certainly not as a part of their essence, or as an accident, but as an agent is present to the thing in which it acts."[81] God is in things as an agent and a final cause is in something, not as a part of their composition. He is not the subject or potential from which they are made (material cause), nor is he a part of their substance (formal cause).

When Scripture does use maternal images of God - for instance, "But Zion said, 'The Lord has forsaken me; my Lord has forgotten me.' Can a woman forget her nursing child, that she should have no compassion on the son of her womb? Even these may forget, yet I will not forget you." (Is. 49: 14-15) - it emphasizes the loving care and intimacy of God. But even here, one cannot think of God as immanent unless He is transcendent as the cause. At the end of the passage, God is clearly described as the "Mighty One of Jacob". (Is. 49: 26).

As Manfred Hauke has put it in his book, Women in the Priesthood: "Accordingly, the Old Testament does *not* place the *father and mother symbolisms* for God *next to each other, but* slots them, as it were, *into one another*: the 'mother symbol [inheres] in the father symbol'." [82] The term "father" cannot be discarded or viewed as on an equal footing with the term "mother". Though God does have "maternal" characteristics, these are affirmed of God because his care, his providence, his truth and his love reach from the greatest to the least of his creation through his causality. His causality affirms his transcendence. He is wholly present in creation because he is wholly other. Because in him essence and existence are one, all the essences of whatever exists, whether dogs and cats or electrons, the color yellow or the number of hairs on my head, participate in his existence and thus experience his intimate presence.

If God were just a thing composed like everything else, then he could not enjoy intimacy with everything. He does enjoy such intimacy, not by physical contact, but because his power must be present to them to create them, conserve them in existence and support things in moving back to himself. As St. Thomas explains, "Things without bodies are not in a place by the contact of the dimensions measured by quantity, like a body; but by the contact of power."[83] "By calling God 'Father', the language of faith indicates two main things: that God is the first origin of everything and transcendent authority; and that he is at the same time goodness and loving care for all his children."[84]

Though God cares for his creation and is intimately involved in it, He is not changed or modified in the act of creating. (A number of years ago the Dominicans held a Thomistic Congress in Berkeley and a famous Dominican dogmatic theologian told the assembly that if theologians wanted really to relate to the modern world, they just had to admit that God could change. Most were hearing this idea for the first time in their lives.)

In fact, St. Thomas explains how God can be father without origin and still be intimate to his creation. Creation is not a change but a relation. This term abstracts from change. In creation, something which did not exist which was nothing, comes to exist by the power of God. There is no real relation between God and the world. All things absolutely depend on him. But, in fact, there is a real relation between the world and God. We imagine a relation between God and the world because this is the only way we can conceive of creation. But this relation is only in our mind.[85]

To the term "father", which is generally ascribed to God in the Old Testament to manifest his transcendence and immanence to creation, the New Testament adds a new dimension - a Trinitarian dimension. The term "father" could be used to express merely the transcendence of God as creator, which of course it does express. But, in the New Testament it takes on an additional and more profound meaning. Father also has the sense of Unbegotten. The father is not a Son. Yet the Son is begotten. We pray to Christ as Only-begotten. This could mean that Jesus is not transcendent like the Father.

Of course, this is an ancient heresy. Christ, the prime revealer and revelation of the Father, addresses this dilemma himself in the New Testament. The expression from the Old Testament is preserved when Christ refers to the Jews as the children of God. He uses "your Father" or "thy father" fifteen times in the Sermon on the Mount and five times in the rest of Matthew's Gospel. He uses the term "my Father", once at the end of the Sermon and no fewer than nineteen times in the rest of the Gospel. His relationship with God is special and expressed by the proper name "Father" which also means unbegotten, but not in the same way as God is Unbegotten in relation to creation. "Jesus revealed that God is Father in an unheard of sense: he is Father not only in being Creator; he is eternally Father by his relationship to his only Son who reciprocally, is Son only in relation to his Father."[86]

The term "Father" as Jesus uses it is a proper name to express the difference between the Father and the Son. Both the persons share the same essence. They are both God. If Father is used to express the essence of God, and the Son is not the Father, then the Son would be not God, but created. This was of course the objection of Arius, the heretic, to referring to the Son as God. If Father expresses the action of the Father towards the Son, then the Son would also be created. Several Fathers of the Church dealt with this difficulty. St. Gregory Nazianzus says: "O men so subtle! The name of Father signifies neither essence nor action but indicates a relation, that which the Father has towards his Son or the Son towards his Father."[87]

St. Thomas is very exact: "The name of Father signifies directly a relation and, obliquely, the essence with which it is identical."[88] The term "Father" within the Trinity refers to difference in "relation of origin". The Father is infinite, eternal, all-powerful, without origin. The Word or Son is infinite, eternal, all-powerful, but receiving origin from the Father.

God is the Father of the Son from eternity, but he is the Father of creation in time. The Fatherhood of God respecting the Son is the paradigm of all fatherhood and prior in understanding to all human fatherhood. The present attempt to reduce all personal relations in God to some innocuous term expressing their actions, like Creator,

Redeemer or Sanctifier, completely destroys the unique relationship of the Father and the Son and also empties Christianity of the central mystery of faith.

In fact, all the actions outside of the Trinity are done by all three of the persons. Though we attribute the actions to one or another, this is only in our understanding. To have a complete idea of creation, the order between the persons must be preserved. For example, to the affirmation that the Father is creator, one must add that the Son is *Creator genitus* (begotten creator) and the Holy Spirit is *Creator procedens* (proceeding Creator).[89]

The persons in God have an eternal relationship which involves complete interest, complete union, complete action and yet complete distinction. They are the paradigm for all personal relationships on earth. It follows that the relation between the Father and the Son is also the model for all human fatherhood based on the exercise of authority in truth, love and benevolence.

The affirmation of the supreme benevolence and care of God the Father as both the creator and the Father of Jesus Christ serves as a model for the recovery of the true idea of human fatherhood in the face of the excessive egalitarianism of the modern world. The father is the head of the wife as Christ is the head of the Church. The motto which must underlie this is, "To serve is to reign." Obedience and love are perfectly connected because of the will. Obedience has to do the will of another; love is a union of wills. The father and mother have an order of service between them and both have an order of service to God. Each must be perfected by love.

The father shares in God's role as creator. Marriage is a creative act intimately related to bringing forth life. This life is ordered to God. Even Aristotle said, "There is something divine about the human seed."[90] The purpose of the sharing of seed is the bringing forth of the personal spiritual life of a human being. The reason a human being exists is to experience communion with God. This is brought to him in the baptismal font, the second regeneration or rebirth. As the soul is the life of the body, so God is the life of the soul.

The marriage union is a creative union. The order of authority which the father initiates cannot be completely perfected without the truth and love which accompanies all of God's creation and the total commitment and intimacy with the mother and the children which the creator enjoys with all creation. Here we can see that the reduction of marriage to mere power or sexual pleasure is like eating the peel and throwing away the banana. In procreation, both the father and mother participate in a divine action. They therefore act on behalf of God. The father and mother supply the matter and God directly creates the form. This means they must allow the creator his rights and look on what they are doing as a holy act. In the old marriage rite the parties used to say, "With my body I thee worship." The participation of man and woman in the act of procreation is a form of worship and in Christ becomes an image of him.

The father perfects his image as creator only in being a true lover and love here does not mean physical desire, nor just a storm of emotion as in romantic love, though emotion is not ruled out. The fullness of the meaning of love here involves sacrifice for others. "Greater love than this has no man, than to offer his life for his friends." Christ showed obedience and love in his perfect sacrifice. Marriage is the greatest natural friendship among men. In Christ, it becomes an image of his dying on the cross for us. The strength of the man does not exist to take, but to give and protect. The reasoning forces in man are not for the purpose of manipulation and use, but to affirm and draw the good out of others. The father must look on his wife and children not as "them", but as "myself". A friend is a second self and the love of marriage redeemed by grace is especially drawn to such an offering.

Though it is true to say that wives must obey their husbands as Christ, this does not mean that they are slaves submissive to a tyrant. The obedience of a wife is nothing other than the love of a wife, implemented in her desire to rest secure in the strength of her husband. Thomas Aquinas tells us that obedience and love go together because they both involve a union of wills. The obedience of wife to husband parallels that of free citizen to wise governor as they are equals in human dignity.

If a husband is a moral derelict, he has no inner strength on which a wife can rely. His manliness is increased in direct proportion to the extent that he can help her flower into full womanhood by giving herself freely as a person because she relies on him to do the same. Here is true power and benevolence. If he looks on her as existing only to stoke his ego, or if he becomes a tyrant, it is no wonder that she rebels. Women are not as interested in mere material support as they are in emotional and more importantly moral support. She must truly feel loved, wanted and needed in the relationship. The money in the family is not his money. They are one flesh. Whatever is held is held by the two as one.

The family is a domestic Church. Because both parents are baptized they participate in Christ as priest, prophet and king through the baptismal character, which is a true change in their souls. Both parents fulfill their priestly character in teaching the truth and offering the sacrifice of themselves for each other. This is the cornerstone of the priesthood of the laity and the place where it is principally exercised. In religion, this teaching is done much more by an attitude of being than by action. The holiness of the priest centers around the Mass and prayer; in the same way, fatherhood must be realized in leading the family in prayer. For example, a father might take the children to Mass. Perhaps they could sit in front and the father could quietly explain each part of the ritual to the child.

Both parents must participate in nourishing the baptismal character of one another. They are priests to each other. The same is true of the children. Everyone helps everyone else to get to heaven. The father is the head of the family liturgical community. In homes where the father has chosen not to exercise this role, there is no spiritual leader. St. Augustine used to address fathers of families as "My fellow bishops . . ."

The parents exercise their priestly roles in preparing the children to get to heaven. This includes the role of education. Children do not have developed intellects and wills and so must be guided to the truth. The influence of both parents is necessary. The mother's is especially important in primary years, but the father's becomes especially necessary in adolescence. When men absent themselves from this task because they are too busy, the children suffer greatly.

The father establishes the norm for humanity. In an egalitarian age, no wonder masculinity is reduced to fast guns, fast cars, fast fists and fast men and women. The father should be the primary hero in the child's life. Instead, all our heroes are judged by their ability to use guns, fists, basketballs or women. If education is primarily an education in virtue as the ancients believed, the father must take first place in this by himself being a virtuous man and caring enough to lead others as far as they can go in developing this.

Today, in many homes, both parents are breadwinners. Still, women always feel the tug of the home, which is their natural domain despite being paid good salaries for work outside the home. Both parents look on their primary role today as being the one who brings home the paycheck. This is largely because the Industrial Revolution moved work outside the home. In fact, the paycheck is the modern equivalent of the obligation to provide for the material well being of the family. But this will do no good without spiritual breadwinning also. Christ asked, "What father would give his son a stone if he asked for bread?" When fathers allow their work as material breadwinners to cut them off from the family, they are feeding the family with stones instead of bread.

Charles Peguy called heads of families, "The great adventurers of the modern world." No action hero faces a greater challenge than the responsibility for the formation of souls in the face of the secularism of the modern world. The fathers and mothers are the priests who bring the world to God so that the ministerial priests can bring God to the world.

For this purpose, every father must practice the counsels of poverty, chastity and obedience according to what is appropriate for his vocation. Poverty is lived by self-abnegation in serving the family and not giving into the mad pursuit of material wealth; chastity, as respect for his wife as a person, even including periodic continence if necessary to deepen and sharpen sexuality as a true affirmation of the other as human and precious in God's eyes; obedience, as the attempt to implement divine providence in the lives of the members of the family. His prayer should not be, "My will be done in heaven as it is on earth", but "Thy will be done on earth in the family as it is in heaven." Homes as domestic churches are a school for charity in which the father teaches best by example. When St. Augustine was converted by St. Ambrose, he is reputed to have said, "I am not convinced by your arguments, but by the great love you show me."

The father increases in sanctity as an icon of God the Father to the extent that he offers all in surrender to the providence of God and gives himself to the good of his family. Then he is a true *alter Christus*, another Christ. Contraception is the direct antithesis of all these mysteries. It reduces all the others to a cipher of self and one's own pleasure. Is it any wonder that the world is filled with spiritual and emotional frustration, a frustration that is rooted first and foremost in the destruction of the family? Contraception turns children and spouses into objects of use for self. This is the direct antithesis of the personalistic norm and the Trinitarian dimension of the family. When everyone manipulates each other, the only result is power without benevolence.

A beautiful expression of human fatherhood is found in Homer's Iliad. The Trojan hero Hector is about leave the city to fight the Greek hero Achilles. He will be killed in the fight. His wife Andromache bids him farewell, saying, "Hector, you are to me all in one: father, venerable mother, and brother, you are my husband in the prime of your life." A woman hopes to find in her husband all the strength, affection and companionship she found in the home she left.

Douglas MacArthur, the great General of World War II and Korea, once said, "By profession I am a soldier and take pride in the fact. But I am prouder—infinitely prouder—to be a father. A soldier destroys in order to build; the father only builds never destroys. The one has the potentiality of death; the other embodies creation and life. And while hordes of death are mighty, the battalions of life are mightier still. It is my hope that my son, when I am gone, will remember me not from battle but in the home repeating our simple daily prayer, 'Our Father Who Art in Heaven.'"

Chapter 4
THE BODY AND SOUL OF THE HUMAN ACT

The basic theme of this book is that man is made in the image of God and ordered to heaven in both his body and his soul. So far, I have applied this truth to the problem of human destiny, to the concept of man as a person and to the practical implications of these truths for vocations like human fatherhood. Moral life is central to all these questions because free choice is the way man arrives at heaven. In fact, matter and form or body and soul of the human act are key concepts in the truth of a moral judgement.

Modern philosophy has a tendency to divorce body from soul. This divorce affects our ability to gauge the truth of free choices in arriving at heaven. The "body and soul" of the human act are terms which are used analogously when applied to morals. Just as many people today have difficulty examining the necessary connection of matter to spirit in man, so modern moralists have difficulty determining the exact relation of objective human acts done with the body or the other powers of man to the inner intention of man (the soul of the act, so to speak). Just how do exterior acts perfect my soul so that by my free choices I can arrive at heaven?

According to traditional Catholic moral theology, each free choice a man makes has three bases on which it can be judged good or evil. "The morality of human acts depends on: - the object chosen; -the end in view or intention; - the circumstances of the action. The object, the intention, and the circumstances make up the 'sources', or constitutive elements, of the morality of human acts."[91] These are respectively, the action itself, the things that surround it, including the consequences, and the personal or individual motive that inspired it. Each of these elements can have a moral meaning, so all three must be morally good for an action to be morally good. "A *morally good* act requires the goodness of the object, of the end and of the circumstances together."[92] But, the modern school does not accept this. Just as modern philosophy divorces matter from form, so modern morals divorces the material part of an act from the formal part. The object (material) is treated as neutral to the intention and circumstances (formal).

The divorce of the material object of a moral act from the formal inner meaning is at the root of a position which has much influence in contemporary Moral Theology, called "moderate teleology" also known as "consequentialism", or "proportionalism". This tendency to interpret all actions as morally indifferent – as a moral cadaver (neutral) - until motive and circumstances are applied is also represented in the theory of the "fundamental option". These theories are well expressed by one of their principal proponents, Fr. Richard McCormick, S.J., in his response to the papal encyclical Veritatis Splendor.

> That brings us to one of the tendencies that concerns that Pope: proportionalism. . . . He [John Paul II] cites as an objection to proportionalist tendencies the notion that some acts are intrinsically evil from their object. I believe all proportionalists would admit this *if the object is broadly understood as including all the morally relevant circumstances.*
>
> In conclusion, proportionalists are not justifying "deliberate choices of kinds of behaviour [sic] contrary to the commands of the divine and natural law ". They are saying that we must look at all dimensions (morally relevant circumstances) before we know what the action is and whether it should be said to be "contrary to the commands of the divine and natural law".[93]

Though what McCormick says about morally relevant circumstances has been true of determining good actions, it has never been true concerning evil actions. Since *bonum ex integra causa* (good comes from an integral cause), no act can finally be determined as good until the object, intention and circumstances are considered. A defect on any level would make an act evil. Thus, traditionally speaking, the object of a given act should not be considered "broadly"[94]. The object should be considered strictly as:

> a good toward which the will deliberately directs itself. It is the matter of a human act. The object chosen morally specifies the act of the will, insofar as reason recognizes and judges it to be or not to be in conformity with the true good.[95]

Therefore, "there are acts which, in and of themselves, *independently of circumstances* and intentions, are always gravely illicit by reason of their object; such as blasphemy and perjury, murder and adultery."[96][Italics added] These acts are the "matter", or subjects, that receive the action of the will, in which the person may have his own agenda when choosing the act. That agenda is irrelevant to the consideration of the evil of the object.

Like the modern separation of body from spirit, this separation of the matter and form in human acts results in a divorce of morals from nature. When human choices fulfill nothing about human powers, then morals does not perfect nature. The key concept in this divorce of the material from the formal in morals is that of nature. What is the difference between nature and morals? Traditionally, the natural law has been the basis for determining the morality of physical deeds that are open to the direction and use of human freedom. "The Church has often made reference to the Thomistic doctrine of natural law, including it in her own teaching on morality."[97] The modern problem stems from a real objection to the use of the natural law in ethics.

For modern theologians, this whole idea of the natural law suggests the physicalism or biologism of the Eighteenth Century. In other words, natural law would seem the same as the fixed laws of nature stemming from Newtonian Physics, which guided Enlightenment thinkers to posit a determination in human acts similar to the absolute determination which they mistakenly believed they could find in nature. Moral norms, which were looked on as matter for human acts and were based on this idea of the natural law, would be little better than denials of human freedom. As Pope John Paul II remarks in Veritatis Splendor, "*Other moralists*, however, in their concern to stress the importance of values, remain sensitive to the dignity of freedom, but they frequently conceive of freedom as somehow in opposition to or in conflict with material and biological nature, over which it must progressively assert itself."[98]

Man is at the same time "both a servant and free".[99] This text from St. Augustine is an excellent summary of the traditional Catholic teaching on moral theology. Since the Second Vatican Council, many theologians claim that the traditional systematic approach of Catholic theology before the Council, which emphasizes man's service of the natural law coupled with his freedom as a Person, could not now be sustained. Karl Rahner, for example, speaks about the possibility of writing a fundamental catechism, which would be valid for the whole world, in very disparaging terms arguing that one can no longer make any universal statements which are valid for the whole human race. This would include the natural law.

> In order to show the impossibility of a single, new, basic and universal credal statement we may perhaps call attention first of all to the fact that attempts to create a common and universally valid world catechism

> and to introduce it officially have collapsed, and have met with the unambiguous resistance of both preachers and catechists. This is true despite the fact that there was once an official tridentine catechism ...[100]

Nowhere is this malaise in determining a universally valid theology more evident than in moral theology. The great variety of opinions on the foundation of morals has led to a dizzying skepticism on the part of many moralists as to whether absolute moral norms exist. So great has this skepticism become, that Pope John Paul II felt called to write an encyclical, Veritatis Splendor, on the subject of absolutes in morality. This would have been unnecessary before Vatican II.

Great outcry from moral theologians greeted Veritatis Splendor. Many assumed the Pope was trying to turn back the clock to the times before Vatican II, while others ridiculed the encyclical as a feeble attempt to beat the dead horse of birth control. One reader's reaction:

> After reading the new papal encyclical carefully, I felt greatly discouraged. Several hours later I suffered long-lasting seizures of the brain, and looked forward hopefully to leaving the Church on earth for the Church in heaven. After regaining my normal brain function, however, I have a new feeling of confidence, without blinding my eyes and heart to the pain and brain-convulsions that are likely to ensue in the immediate future.[101]

Sadly, many involved in this dispute do not realize that the problem of human nature is integrally involved in the relationship of the soul to the body. Instead, they accept a theory of moral norms which looks upon the object of acts as physical matter on which the spirit works through free will in a completely extrinsic manner. This hearkens back to the old "man in the machine" concept of the human soul. The contraceptive mentality, for instance, looks on babies and the body as material which one can use indifferently for self-satisfying purpose, as a craftsman uses wood to shape any vessel he pleases. In this view, there is no intrinsic relation between the person and the action which he performs with his body.

Some criticized Veritatis Splendor by arguing that all attempts to classify human actions by absolute norms should be viewed with suspicion. No universal statement can express a complete truth, they said, in morals or life in general. Thus, any attempt to classify moral actions is bound to fail; the conscience must give the final solution to the problem.

This lack of confidence in universal laws to express moral truths, especially when dealing with actions of the body like sexuality, has led not only to the destruction of the whole idea of natural law as the basis for morals, but also to a minimalism in confessional practice and a loss of hope that anyone can really lead a life of virtue based on grace.

The classic source for the error in metaphysics and epistemology that has led to this strange break with tradition must be attributed to Karl Rahner, whose ideas about nature were inadequate to say the least. Though Rahner tried to defend the truth of absolute universal statements against writers like Hans Küng, his idea of essences is sadly unequal to this task.

> Rahner took issue with Kung and attempted to refute Kung's thesis that the Church could not define infallibly because no human statement could be absolutely true, arguing instead that the judgement does take the mind to reality. While we have seen how Rahner argued to this conclusion, we have also seen that there is an inherent weakness within his

> thought. [...] [I]t is not transparently clear how conceptual thought in Rahner's own epistemological system can be preserved from relativisation.[102]

Rahner reflects his idea that universals seem to be impoverished sense experiences in his teaching about the application of moral laws. He divides ethics into two sciences, one of which is essentialist and material. This is the science of the universal moral norms. The other is the existentialist and formal. This is the place where the conscience actually judges the moral truth of a specific action. The material essentialist ethics teaches us generally what we are to do. Humanae Vitae and the Commandments could be considered examples of material essentialist ethics; they are like recommendations, for such general rules cannot express the complete individuality of the person in anything.

> Anyone, however, who can grasp this holistic thought of something real which cannot be subsumed unequivocally under a universal idea or under a law, cannot reject the idea from the very start that something like this is conceivable – indeed, must be postulated – also in man as a spiritual person, as that existent who does not resolve himself completely into *forma-materia-esse.*[103]

Since no universal law can apply in all cases, Rahner holds that a formal existential system of ethics expresses the conscience and discernment of the Holy Spirit in individual cases. "If the creative will of God is directly and unambiguously directed to the concrete and the individual, then surely this is not merely true in so far as this individual reality is the realization of a case of the universal – rather it is directed to the concrete as such, as it really is –

to the concrete in its positive, and particularly its substantial, material uniqueness."[104]

To describe this new system of an "individual norm"[105] that will complement the science of universal norms, Rahner coins the term "existential ethics". "The notion of an 'existential ethics' . . . shows itself unequivocally the counter – and the complementary notion of an abstractly universal 'essentialist' ethics."[106] The discernment of the Holy Spirit is necessary in each case and can contradict the universal law.

Rahner thus teaches that there are two systems of ethics, one material, the other formal. The material aspect of human acts is treated as though it were always indifferent matter, out of which the moral will makes what it pleases in absolute freedom. Though it is true that the will is the formal principle in moral freedom, still the material goods are not morally indifferent before the individual intention and circumstances come into play. And a good will cannot change the intrinsic meaning of an act itself as it relates to human nature. The Pope makes clear that in regard to birth control neither the child nor the parents are inert tools, like wood, malleable to any use. Each has a unique nature made in the image of God. Each has a spirit that transcends matter in the use of the body, for emotions and physical acts express the spirit of composite man. Though many emotional and physical acts may be indifferent in relation to the will, some certainly would not be appropriate subject matter for a human act. Man could not realize his freedom in a good way and get to heaven using these acts.

Because man is made in the image of God, material acts that regard bringing new human beings into the world cannot be merely indifferent in relation of reason. Further, human beings have the purpose of eternal unity with God, so no action that regards bringing them into being can be made without reference to God for whom they are destined. Vatican II clearly expressed two aspects of norms which befit persons: first, no human being can be an object of use, but must be a subject of love. Second, human beings only find their true fullness in a sincere giving of themselves to others. The supreme example of self-giving is found in marriage and bringing children into the world. Any material manipulations of man which regard reproduction would be inappropriate. Reason teaches this and demands that in these cases the matter be truly proportioned to the form of the will – as truth expresses love.

There cannot be two sciences of morals because matter and form, the essential and the existential, go together. If they did not, truth and love would have no material expression in man.

Chapter 5
O LIFE BY WHICH I LIVE!

> A great portent appeared in heaven, a woman clothed with the sun, with the moon under her feet, and on her head a crown of twelve stars; she was with child and she cried out in her pangs of birth, in anguish for delivery. And another portent appeared in heaven; behold, a great red dragon, with seven heads and ten horns, and seven diadems upon his head. . . . And the dragon stood before the woman who was about to bear a child, that he might devour her child when she brought it forth. (Rev. 12:1-4)

There are many applications of matter and form, or body and soul, in moral discourse. This is especially true of issues concerning the right to life. The divorce of the matter from form in these areas is at the root of the culture of death in which we live. We see this in the description of the war between the woman and the dragon in the Book of Revelation.

The dragon and the woman about to bear a child are two images for deep currents of life. The pregnant woman represents all aspects of human life. These aspects include the natural life of man as an existing being (Eve and Adam), together with the supernatural completion of that life which Christ brings to us in grace (Mary and Christ). The dragon, here invoked in the last book of the Bible, puts us in mind of the serpent-tempter in the Bible's first book. That serpent tempted man to act without the aid of God, the life by which we live. In sin, then, death - and the whole culture of death - was introduced into the human race. In this culture, which rivals the culture of life, life becomes not gift, but possession, a possession over which man has the absolute freedom spoken of in the last chapter. Man embraces himself as the only life by which he lives, denying the central sovereignty of God. He thus experiences both spiritual (moral) and physical death.

In C.S. Lewis' popular work, The Screwtape Letters, a senior tempter in Hell meditates on the nature of Hell for the benefit of a younger tempter on earth.

> The whole philosophy of Hell rests on the recognition of the axiom that one thing is not another thing and, specially, that one self is not another self. My good is my good, your good is yours. What one gains another loses. Even an inanimate object is what it is by excluding all other objects from the space it occupies . . . 'To be' *means* 'to be in competition.'
>
> Now the Enemy's philosophy is nothing more nor less than one continued attempt to evade this very obvious truth. He aims at a contradiction. Things are to be many, yet somehow one. The good of one self is the good of another. This impossibility He calls *Love*, and this same monotonous panacea can be detected under all He does and even all He is - or claims to be. Thus He is not content, even Himself, to be a sheer arithmetical unity; He claims to be three as well as one, in order that this nonsense about Love might find a foothold in His own nature. At the other end of the scale, He introduces into matter that obscene invention the organism, in which the parts are perverted from their natural destiny of competition and made to cooperate.[107]

In his encyclical Evangelium Vitae (The Gospel of Life), Pope John Paul II gives an impressive analysis of how things can be many and yet one, and explains how the order of reason must be preserved in material, physical acts of the body which concern life. This happens through human life, both physical and spiritual, for all life reflects the life by which we live, that is, God. God is the most living thing. Indeed, God is not a living thing but life itself. This is because God exists in Himself. He receives nothing from anything or anyone else which he does not have. He is not one as a unit of measurement, but he is one because he is all. His diversity is perfect and pure society in which all the persons of the Blessed Trinity pour themselves out to one another in gift and reception and joy. "Life in the highest degree belongs properly in God. . . a thing is said to live in so far as it operates of itself and not as moved by another." [108] Complete interior life and complete communion characterize the unity and diversity of God. All things must imitate Him.

> We must celebrate Eternal Life, from which every other life proceeds. From this, in proportion to its capacities, every being which in any way participates in life, receives life. Every life and every living movement proceed from this life which transcends all life and every principle of life.[109]

All things come forth from the one life who is God and in their great diversity seek to return to the one life who is God. The source of this movement is divine love. The manner of return is acting according to divine truth. "But even the particle of inanimate matter 'desires' and 'loves' (is attracted to) another particle. Gravity is low-level love; love is very high-level gravity."[110]

Every being seeks unity. Beings without life are too tenuous in existence actually to experience unity from their multiplicity. Rocks collide and break apart, but the unity of a heap of stones is a unity more in name than in fact. When the threshold of organic life is passed, real unity in diversity becomes possible. This is because the organism is the most basic thing which participates in life. A thing is living insofar as the source by which it moves is found within it. "To live" means not "to be in competition" but "to be in cooperation".

Self-movement is certainly found in the cell division of the most basic of organisms. The plant takes the sun, the earth, the air, water and nutrients from the soil and unifies them in organic life, which is characterized by growth and reproduction. Yet plant unity is also a deficient unity. In the simplest division of a cell, the organism must destroy the beings which are united within it to change them into tissue. Thus, self-movement is not movement toward real unity with another thing, but a destruction of other things to change them into a new organism. The sun, earth, air and water change into the organism, but to their own peril. Perhaps this is why many think that life involves competition. This tenuous hold on life is very fleeting, indeed. After all, the lilies of the field pass away very quickly. Every autumn the leaves change color and fall from the trees.

A greater degree of self-movement and interior integration can be seen in animals. Animals not only have organic life, but they can also experience other individual things interiorly without destroying them. They do this by the five senses, by interior sense-powers of knowing like memory and imagination, and by their emotions. An animal can experience a tree, a plant, another animal or its master. In this experience the animal must unify many sense impressions to experience within itself something that exists outside itself. The animal experiences a unity with other things not only through knowledge, but also through emotional life. A cat or dog has intense individual experiences of unity with other things. Still, the animal cannot surpass unity with particular trees, rocks, plants or masters. The animal is imprisoned in the particular thing that it can sense, and a unity with all things is impossible for it. Life is very limited, then, by the walls of the actual things the animal has experienced. The animal has imagination but no creativity. The animal can remember, but not reminisce about memory and live in another time and another place.

Man is the only being who can actually arrive at unifying all things by knowing them in his intelligence and loving them with his will. In this ability, the living human soul surpasses all other things and is not just a trace of God, but an image of God, who is Life itself.

> It is to this that souls owe their incorruptibility; and because of this all animals and plants live, which receive only the faintest glimmer of life. To men, beings made of spirit and matter, Life grants life. Even if we should abandon Life, because of its overflowing love for man, it converts us and call us back to itself.[111]

Man exhibits his characteristic life in spiritual acts which lead him to posit the existence of the spiritual powers of intellect and will, which in turn must be rooted in a spiritual soul. Every human being reflects the very image of the Very Life which is God in his own existence, whether he manifests acts of intellect and will or not. No physical organism could produce this spirit. Man is not just a complex animal, but possesses a spirit completely above matter. For this reason, Thomas Aquinas says that each act of sexual sin is extremely serious because human seed does not and can never have a merely material purpose.

> Man is a king. Created to exercise dominion over the world, he was given the likeness to the king of the universe; he is the living image who participates by his dignity in the perfection of the divine archetype.[112]

Since the soul of man is made in the image and likeness of the king of the universe, then "in man's seed there is something divine, because it is man potentially."[113]

The Gospel of life, then, is founded on the very nature of man. This Gospel of life is not just a reaction of the Church against certain negative practices of secular society. Rather, this Gospel of life is a positive affirmation of human life in all its splendor, a life which comes from the hand of a good God, reflects that good God in every interior act, and must return to the good God who is Life Itself.

> Not only this: it promises to bring us, body and soul to perfect life, to immortality. It is too little to say that this life is alive: it is the Principle of Life, the Cause and sole Wellspring of life. Every living thing must contemplate it and gives it praise: it is Life which overflows with Life.[114]

The treatment of life in Evangelium Vitae is divided into four chapters. After a brief introduction, the Pope takes up the problem of modern-day threats to life. This takes the form of a commentary on the story of Cain and Abel in Genesis. In the second chapter, the Pope speaks of human life on all levels as a gift which is given man by God. He analyses it from the standpoint of the principle, model, and purpose or goal of all human life that is the inner nature of God. In the third chapter, the Pope examines the implications of respect for the divine image in man which are expressed by the commandments. This respect is applied to the divine, the natural and the civil law. Abortion and euthanasia are specifically treated here as violations of this image on all three levels. Finally, the Pope offers some positive practical steps for nourishing the divine image in man, particularly in the family and among women, where the attack against life seems more immediate and pressing in contemporary society. The encyclical ends with a discussion of Mary, who is the "mother of life" and the example in nourishing life on every level in man.

The Pope begins this encyclical by first establishing its urgency. The value of every human life, he explains, is beyond price because of "its supernatural calling"[115]. Yet that same life is attacked practically every day, in most societies, by such practices as abortion and euthanasia. If this were not enough, government practices in this regard seem to be eroding the very conscience of man itself. This conscience, "darkened as it were by such widespread conditioning, is finding it increasingly difficult to distinguish between good and evil in what concerns the basic value of human life."[116] The urgency of making a "precise and vigorous affirmation of the value of human life and its inviolability"[117] has given rise to this encyclical, which is not solely the Pope's initiative, but the fruit of collaboration with all the bishops of the world.

This present-day crisis is merely a symptom, albeit a particularly graphic one, of a crisis as old as the human race itself. It is the crisis of the "eclipse of the value of life"[118] which has afflicted the human race since the murder of Abel. What is new is that murder has now become a "right" and is no longer regarded as a crime, especially when it attacks the weakest members of society. This has given rise to a global and social structure of systematic sin, applauded and perpetrated by state and health care institutions. The Pope calls this system "the culture of death".[119] In its many aberrations concerning human life, not only is the death of the innocent not considered murder, but "the life which could result from a sexual encounter . . . becomes an enemy to be avoided at all costs."[120]

The source of this mortal culture is the "Promethean attitude which leads people to think that they can control life and death."[121] Whether the issue is fetal experimentation, euthanasia, abortion, or questions of overpopulation, the philosophical root is always the same: "a perverse idea of freedom"[122] that carries "subjectivity to the extreme."[123] Since man experiences a freedom in his acts, modern man has carried this experience to an illogical extreme, arguing that freedom has only rights, not duties.[124] Modern man and the culture of death "exalt freedom to such an extent that it becomes an absolute"[125]and therefore the human conscience becomes a law unto itself.

The Pope calls this idea "a completely individualistic concept of freedom"[126] which destroys all respect for rights among men and leads men, in imitation of Cain, to claim that they are not their brother's keeper. In truth, man possesses an "inherently relational dimension",[127]for he is naturally social. This inherent social solidarity begins first with God and descends to relate all men to one another in a bond of mutual respect, expressed by the fact that freedom must have "an essential link with truth."[128] But, when the essential link with the truth of human nature is lost, a relativism of truth results, and this relativism makes democracy a competition for goods without regard for any but the powerful. Since it denies any standard outside the human subjective conscience as the arbiter of good and evil, such democracy, by implication, connotes an atheistic secularism. In fact, the relativising of truth is based on the loss of the sense of God. "The values of *being* are replaced by those of *having*."[129]

This relativism has become so pervasive that it affects even Catholic circles and institutions. Those who divorce the actions of the soul from the body have strange reactions to death. First, they have almost no concept of an afterlife or the resurrection of the dead. They identify the next life with the colored lights and altered states of consciousness described by many New Age writers. Never mind that common sense should tell them that a personal encounter with the risen Lord and the persons of the Trinity ought to be more than colored lights and music. Many will say that the fact that someone (for example, one who has survived an out-of-body experience) has come back from the dead completely discounts the Gospel accounts of the appearances of the risen Lord.

Another misunderstanding is the statement that a comatose patient is "not the same person" anymore. Presumably this would mean that being a Person results from an I-Thou relationship with the reporting individual and actual expression of this relationship. Thus, a person who cannot communicate as he used to is "not the same person". Never mind that he has measurable brain waves.

Christ reverses this moral relativism by shedding His blood so the shedding of innocent blood might cease. He sprinkles his blood in imitation of Abel, but His blood "speaks more eloquently than the blood of Abel," (Heb. 12:24) for, "the blood of Abel cries for vengeance, but the blood of Christ cries for pardon"[130] because it "consists in a sincere gift of self."[131]

The Pope sees, in all levels of society and families, positive signs of the confrontation of the "culture of death" with the "culture of life" which is the result of the action of Christ. The Gospel of life, which is pro-life in itself, encourages, supports and proclaims these positive signs. These signs help us to learn that life is a rich gift to us and that therefore we must give it to others by respecting their inherent right to life.

In the second chapter, the Pope explains why this life cannot submit to mere moral relativism or competition, basing his argument on the source and purpose of human life. Christ has shown us this purpose in all of his actions and sufferings, and it is precisely to nourish this human life that Christ came. Though formed of the dust of the earth, man "is a manifestation of God in the world, a sign of his presence, a trace of his glory."[132] As St. Irenaeus puts in the famous text that forms the central theme of this book, "Man, fully alive, is the glory of God."[133]

Only God can be the beginning of human life because of the immortality of the soul. Man stands at the summit of material creation because he is the only material being with a spirit. As man comes forth from God, so he must return to God. This means that the destiny of man must be supernatural. Man is called to intimacy with the Trinity, an intimacy completed in seeing God face to face in heaven. The soul is the beginning of life, which animates the body and must be created by God. The Vision of God in heaven is the completion of life and can only be attained by means of grace. "As the soul is the life of body, so God is the blessed life of man."[134] The destiny of natural life in man is eternal life, this vision to be enjoyed in both the soul and the body. This is the foundation for belief in the resurrection of the dead.

> *Here the Christian truth about life becomes most sublime.* The dignity of this life is linked not only to its beginning, to the fact that it comes from God, but also to its final end, to its destiny of fellowship with God in knowledge and love of him. In light of this truth Saint Irenaeus qualifies and completes his praise of man: 'the glory of God' is indeed, 'man, living man', but ' the life of man consists in the vision of God.'[135]

From both the point of view of his creation and the point of view of his destiny, man cannot think he is the sole lord of his own life; the freedom of human life is in no sense absolute. This includes the "freedom" of giving life to others, because God cooperates with a married couple to bring forth "images of God"[136] or "little trinities". All of the events of Scripture testify to the fact that the dominion of man over life is a participated dominion. He receives his life from God and must give it back to God. As God's gift, it must be respected. "Man is not the master of life, nor is he the master of death."[137]

The culmination of the Scriptural doctrine about life is the Cross, where the direction and respect for human life witnessed in Scripture finds its true completion. Since man's life is a participated dominion, on the cross he finds the great truth that *"life finds its center, its meaning and its fulfillment when it is given up."*[138]

In the third chapter of The Gospel of Life, the Pope applies to practical respect for life the great truths he has taught in the letter's initial chapters. This is the true heart of the encyclical, evidenced by the pontiff's solemn declaration concerning the aberrations exhibited by the culture of death: the taking of human life through abortion and euthanasia.

Three times the Pope "confirms" and, in the case of abortion, also "declares" the basic moral doctrines that are the direct fruit of meditation on the exalted character of human life.[139] The language clearly evokes the teaching of the Second Vatican Council in Lumen Gentium, the Dogmatic Constitution on the Church, Paragraph 25, in which the Council teaches that bishops in union with the Pope "proclaim infallibly the doctrine of Christ", if "in their authoritative teaching concerning matters of faith and morals, they are in agreement that a particular teaching is to be held definitively." The teachings to be so held in this encyclical state that the taking of all innocent human life is "always gravely immoral";[140] that "direct abortion, that is, abortion willed as an end or as a means, always constitutes a grave moral disorder"; [141] and that euthanasia understood as "an act or omission which of itself and by intention causes death with the purpose of eliminating suffering" (always distinct from "aggressive medical treatment" and "methods of palliative care") is "a grave violation of the law of God."[142]

John Paul II carefully distinguishes abortion from self-defense and capital punishment, though he is not in favor of the latter. He states that though the State has a right to punish, given modern prison methods this should "rarely, if almost never" be employed.[143] Capital punishment is a right, but its exercise is imprudent today because it is not the best way insure the value of human life in his opinion. Still, the distinction hinges on the adjective "innocent". Here, as in the Catechism of the Catholic Church, the encyclical affirms the traditional teaching that capital punishment and killing in war are not murder [144] because they do not involve an attack on *innocent* human life.

> Moreover, 'legitimate defense can be not only a right but a grave duty for someone responsible for another's life, the common good of the family or of the State' (CCC #2265). [...] Sometimes [this] involves taking his [the aggressor's] life. In this case, the fatal outcome is attributable to the aggressor whose action brought it about, even though he may not be morally responsible because of the lack of the use of reason.[145]

All the various methods of attack on innocent life are to be condemned as morally reprehensible because the dominion of man over his own life is not absolute, but only "ministerial".[146] Man must recognize this ministerial dimension by submitting his conscience to the truth of the natural law, for in the natural law human conscience finds its most basic responsibility to the truth to receive all innocent human life as a gift. It is in the natural law that one knows that he is "at once both a servant and free."[147]

If this is true for the individual conscience, it must also be true for the state, and especially for democracies. Those who embrace the democratic ideal must realize that it is essentially a means of government and not a philosophical system for determining truth. Democracies must use legislatures and presidents to determine how to aid the cause of life. They cannot in themselves determine right or justice or the right to life. Since they did not create the human soul, they cannot determine that soul's right to life by majority rule. Governments do not create life; they respect it. "Fundamentally, democracy is a 'system' and as such is a means and not an end."[148] All forms of government have a much more limited role than the definition of the entire natural or moral law; rather, they implement the natural law by encouraging respect for the rights of the citizens in external, everyday matters which involve the peace and order of the state. Since rights cannot be recognized in a being which does not have a right to exist, "first and fundamental among these is the inviolable right to life of every innocent human being."[149]

It is true that laws already exist which permits abortion on demand and it may not be possible to restrict the practice of abortion in every case. Civil governments may tolerate the evil of abortion in this case by not punishing it as murder. However, this does not mean there is a right to abortion, nor does the State have the right to fund abortions, as this would no longer merely tolerate but actually promote evil.

> While public authority can sometimes choose not to put a stop to something which-were it prohibited-would cause serious harm, it can never presume to legitimize as a right of individuals- even if they are the majority of the members of society- an offence against other persons caused by the disregard of so fundamental a right as the right to life.[150]

Tolerating the practice of abortion by not punishing it as murder is not the same as considering that abortion is not murder or a sin. This toleration can take place only on the condition (which hopefully can be changed) that a law cannot be passed to prohibit abortion altogether.

Since the right to life is so basic a part of human nature as well as civil law, Catholics have the obligation, by conscientious objection, to oppose any law about abortion or euthanasia that attacks the right to life directly.[151] Though one can vote for a law which restricts abortion on demand, and thus limit the taking of life because one cannot forbid all abortion, one can never cooperate directly in any act which causes either abortion or euthanasia.

Nor can the practice of withdrawing food and water in palliative care be tolerated. Almost any patient can take something by mouth at some time, and if he is unable to do so and unable to tolerate an intravenous needle, then his symptoms can be palliated by oral hygiene (for example, keeping his mouth clean as one does in brushing the teeth or using ice chips to alleviate the sensation of hunger but giving some taste to the mouth).

The Pope concludes this portion of the encyclical by emphasizing that the prohibitions on abortion and euthanasia truly reflect absolute moral norms. While observing these precepts does not contain the fullness of the Gospel, it is the necessary beginning to both eternal life and true freedom. "Only when one stops committing these crimes (and no Christian should commit them), one begins to lift up one's head towards freedom. But this is only the beginning of freedom, not perfect freedom."[152]

In the last chapter of the encyclical, the Pope stresses that the Gospel of Life entails not only avoiding sins against life, but also positively promoting life. This is especially true of ordinary acts of self-giving in the family, and in the charitable works of religious institutes. Health-care personnel bear a special responsibility for promoting life, recognized by the Hippocratic Oath.[153] No act of abortion or euthanasia can be a positive contribution to life. All practical forms must encourage the reception of life as a gift from God and the giving of self as the most evident sign of life. Parents begin this with the disinterested love of children, either their own or those they have adopted. In this gift, the child receives the gift of self and so can learn self-restraining love, which is the basis for all love.

Education and hope are key to changing the culture of death into the culture of life. The Church is interested in this both regarding the individual and regarding the State because the Church is interested in man, a being made in the image of God.

For a model of how life should be received and respected, we may look to Mary. The child she brings forth from her womb, who challenges and is wounded on the cross by the serpent and the dragon, is "the figure of every person, every child, especially the helpless baby whose life is threatened."[154] The dragon or serpent of competition seeks to devour each helpless life with the cry that one who is helpless has no right to exist. This is because the culture of death judges the value of life by its usefulness, not as the gift of loving Creator. God is the life by which we live as created, as elevated to grace and fulfilled in the life of heaven. The Church proclaims that all forms of life are progressive realizations of the image of God in man. For this reason, "the rejection of human life, in whatever form that rejection takes, is really a rejection of Christ."[155] But Christ has promised that in the combat between death and life, life will always triumph.

In the Gospel of Life, John Paul II has clearly taken up the challenge of modern culture. He demonstrates clearly that the beginning, model and purpose of human life are only completed in "the life by which I live". Abortion and euthanasia - and, indeed, any practice which assaults the untouchable character of innocent human life - are the instruments by which the dragon seeks to devour the life of the child which each of us shares. That life exists to be, to love God, and to be happy with Him in heaven. He is the God of 'man fully alive", the God of loveliness who destroys the dragon with the simple truth of the goodness of what human life is meant to be.

O loveliness supreme, and Beauty Infinite
O ever-flowing stream and Ocean of delight;
O Life by which I live, my Truest life above,
To Thee alone I give my undivided love.[156]

Chapter 6
DYING BECAUSE I DO NOT DIE

I live, but not in myself
And I have such hope
That I die because I do not die.[157]

This is the first stanza in a long poem of St. John of the Cross in which the mystic author expresses his longing to see God, a longing that is the central mystery of the Christian life. The Catechism of the Catholic Church places this longing to see God at the very outset of the section that concerns Christian morals; we saw at the beginning of this book that seeing God is the destiny of man.

> The New Testament uses several expressions to characterize the beatitude to which God calls man:[...]. the vision of God: 'Blessed are the pure in heart, for they shall see God', [...]'There we shall rest and see, we shall see and love, we shall love and praise. Behold what will be at the end without end.'[158]

Yet, the relation of death to the vision of God in modern theology is by no means clear. Mistakes about the purpose of life become disastrous when applied to the living of life.

Strangely, considering how ill many of his conclusions correspond to the Roman Catholic tradition, many contemporary ideas about the destiny of human life in modern Catholic theology can be traced to Martin Heidegger. Since philosophy is the handmaid of theology, it was only natural that those who were captivated by the philosophy of Heidegger should seek to apply his ideas to theology. Heidegger's ideas have influenced many theologians, especially Karl Rahner and those who followed him. Though this influence can be perceived in many questions, there is perhaps no question discussed by Rahner and his school in which the influence of Heidegger is more clearly seen than the question of the nature and meaning of human death. These ideas apply to both the death of Christ and our death.[159]

Heidegger and Rahner are not only careful but elegant writers, who express their conclusions in ways that captivate the imagination. Because their ideas are so important for the development of modern attitudes towards death, they will be explored thoroughly here. Nevertheless, the reader should not forget that these attitudes – however poetically expressed - differ significantly from those expressed by John Paul II and other, more orthodox, theologians.

A central idea of Heidegger was his view that our presence in the world seems absurd.[160] This is not surprising, as existentialist philosophers generally hold that there are no real essences in the world. When there is no real objective content to knowledge apart from the contribution of the subject examining his own experience, there can be no meaning to the world apart from the meaning with which the knowing subject invests it. The world makes sense only because I want it to or because I need it to; the world in itself has no truly discernible message. The burden of meaning is completely on the subject. The next step is easy: life seems absurd apart from what I make of it.

Death is perhaps the final expression of this absurdity. If it is difficult for the subject to invest with meaning the world he experiences through the senses, it is even more difficult for him to invest meaning in a world absent from his sense experience, such as the world after death, about which we can know nothing. Man has sense experience of death, but not of anything after death. Though man experiences the need to invest his life with a permanent meaning, the desire to exist perpetually, he also experiences the fact that all men die. Man therefore experiences an insoluble conflict between the need for meaning and the absurdity of nothingness.

Modern theologians have applied this confrontation of absurdity and nothingness in death to the death of Christ. They take the cry, "My God, my God, why have you forsaken me?" as a lament founded on the fear, bewilderment and anguish of a dying Christ who sees no resolution to this seemingly complete destruction of himself. The only possible value of this act could be as an example to us of detachment and faith. Like Christ, they say, we should throw ourselves into the chasm of hopelessness, trusting only that God will somehow resolve this completely contradictory and illogical situation.

For much of modern philosophy and theology, then, making sense of death is the primary experience of human life. Death is illogical; what could life be after it? But Christ's death is the prime exemplar of man's attitude in the face of death. According to the view of modern theologians, Christ's attitude in the face of death is an intellectual anguish and hopelessness. His death in faith means simply shutting his eyes to the seeming contradiction and his hope means that he trusts God will somehow resolve this strange paradox, but without any real idea of how this will take place.

Any understanding of the relation of the body to the soul must take account of death. The true place of death in human destiny is important for a true picture of the body and the soul and ultimately to interpret both Christ's death and the death of the Christian.

I. Man is a Being-made-for-death (Sein zum Tode)

> The focus of all anthropological questions, in the sphere of philosophy, is undeniably death, towards which every human being inevitably tends [...] If - as M. Heidegger accurately expressed it - a human being is a 'being-

> towards death', then too an ultimate understanding of the human being becomes more complete when [...] we take into account the moment of death as a fundamental and necessary perspective of human life.[161]

This text from the Lublin existentialist book I-Man very accurately summarizes the place of death in contemporary philosophy. Man is defined as a being-made-for-death. He is a "tauromachus,"[162] a bull in the arena who merely waits for the experience of death to express the meaning and destiny of his life. The attitude of man in the face of this destiny is an anxious freedom. Man stands upright in the face of all the vast emptiness death has to offer and yet embraces it in blackness.

> Anticipation reveals to Dasein (to-ness) its lostness in the they-self, and brings it face to face with the possibility of being itself, primarily unsupported by concernful solicitude, but of being itself, rather, in an impassioned ***freedom towards death*** - a freedom which has been released from the Illusions of the 'they' and which is factical, certain of itself, and anxious.[163]

Man's freedom towards death consists in the fact that death, for Martin Heidegger, is the final destiny of the human race. Ladislas Boros, reflecting on this idea of Heidegger, describes death as "a fundamental modality of living, concrete existence."[164] It is the "perfectio debita" (a due perfection) of all life, including human life.[165] Boros refers to an expression of Heidegger's to illustrate this point. "For example, an unripe fruit develops towards ripeness . . . This 'not yet' is comprised in its own existence, and attains expression in 'ripeness'."[166]

This would suggest that death is the final cause of the whole world. Though it is true that matter tends to corruption, a Catholic might object that only the material part of creation tends to death. One should qualify this analysis, then, with appropriate caveats. Strangely, Boros believes that his statement, which he takes to be Heidegger's, needs qualification also, but in the opposite direction. "True, the presence of death in human existence cannot be grasped from this example without some qualification. It is much *more intensive* (emphasis added), more truly essential, more pervasive."[167] In fact, Boros believes that Heidegger "supplements the comparison (with the fruit ripening) in important respects."[168]

The "important aspects" which Heidegger adds to the comparison include the fact that the fruit has ripening as its fulfillment. Death, however, is not in itself the fulfillment of man. Although Heidegger admits that death is the completion of the life of man, or dasein (to-ness) as he calls man, this is not the end. The experience of the being man consists neither in just resignation to this fate nor in ignoring it, though many do just that. The actual experience of man that distinguishes his death from the death of all other material creation is that man can find meaning and possibility in it. Man is not just a being that dies, but a being-towards-death, a "sein zum Tode". What matters in human death is man's attitude towards it. Death can be considered either a destruction or a possibility; it is the "'anticipation' of this possibility" (vorlaufen in die Möglichkeit) that redeems it.[169] This anticipation can only be truly expressed by anxiety. "*But the state-of-mind which can hold open the utter and constant threat of itself arising from Dasein's own most individualized Being, is anxiety*."[170]

This is the climate in which man realizes his destiny. The freedom towards death of the being-towards-death consists in the anticipation and anxiety of the possibility of non-being or of being everything, accepted realistically and authentically. For Heidegger, the possibility of death is present in every life; only human life involves bravely embracing this possibility and the ability to make something positive of it. The power of man over death lies in his personal decision to undergo it with all of its possibilities.

In fact, Boros maintains this is the only true philosophical attitude towards death. "*Death is man's first completely personal act, and is, therefore, by reason of its very being, the centre above all others for the awakening of consciousness, for freedom, for the encounter with God, for the final decision about one's eternal destiny.*"[171]

All of these ideas come together in systematic form in Karl Rahner's On the Theology of Death, both the source and the summary of his application of Heidegger's ideas on death to Christianity. According to Rahner, when man dies, "his free, personal self-affirmation and self-realization is achieved in death definitively."[172] In death, the soul transcends the limit of its possibility here in this world because it becomes "a-cosmic".[173] Rahner states that even St. Thomas Aquinas says the soul has a transcendental relationship with matter after death, and this is what he means by the soul's becoming a-cosmic. Death in this schema is not merely suffered; it is embraced not only in a biological sense, but in a human existential sense as the final completion of man. Both Rahner and Boros develop their ideas of man's personal self-affirmation as realized in the choice of death by saying that the final decision of death is the only really personal act made by man, working from several comments of St. Thomas Aquinas regarding a text of John Damascene: "Hoc enim est hominibus mors quod est angelis casus. (Death is to man what the fall is to an angel.)"[174] Rahner, for example, comments, "It seems to me - and this is an opinion which can be traced to St. John Damascene and which has the weighty support of St. Thomas - that the finality of the personal life-decision is an intrinsic constituent of death itself as a spiritual and personal act of man."[175]

Boros speaks of the same text in the context of a final decision which man makes. This final decision is made "at the moment of death", which is a moment between clinical death and metaphysical death. One should thus understand *"the final determining of the state after death as having the character of a decision."*[176] Both Boros and Rahner look upon the experience of death as an experience of a final decision that is the summary of all of human life. After all, the angels ended their state of pilgrimage by making one choice; for Boros and Rahner, man ends his state of pilgrimage with one choice.

> The positing of a straightforwardly binding, irreversible decision is so completely connatural to the most intimate aspirations of human liberty even in its decisions before death, that the whole movement of liberty is only possible because in it is anticipated a last, final *prise de position* in regard to absolute value.[177]

It should be plain that this choice for death is a reflection of the Heideggerian anticipation of the possibilities of death. Rahner and Boros go further and maintain that because at the moment of death, one is freed from the influence of the body and its limitations in this life, this personal decision is *"man's first completely personal act"*. Not only is death the only choice and decision, it is also the first complete decision a person ever makes. For that reason, Rahner calls death "both an end and a fulfillment."[178]

The very power of death as fulfillment is based on the attitude of will of the one dying. The "anticipation of the possibilities" which death entails is important to separate the experience of death as a mere empty and hopeless end from death as an experience of faith in union with the death of Christ. The natures of the different experiences of death are distinguished according to the attitude of the subject in approaching death. The very hidden character of what happens after death demands an attitude of will in the dying man that embraces death not as an end, but as a possibility. The attitude of will is essential to death looked upon as a triumph or a tragedy. Furthermore, so that the will may be perfect in this attitude, the afterlife must be shrouded in the anguish and hopelessness of intellectual darkness. If man knows where he is going after death, he cannot be in anguish, for he cannot have the experience of mere possibility. Death in faith demands obscurity.

For man to truly experience death as an occasion of divine grace, it is necessary that man not know what lies beyond death. To die in faith means to have no real knowledge of what happens after death, but to place oneself at the free disposition of God and what God in his own freedom has destined for the individual.

> On account of its obscurity, man should and ought to understand the concrete existential situation of death, in so far as it is his own deed, as the culmination of that anticipatory attitude (a prefiguration of faith) in which man surrenders himself and what that sovereign liberty of God may, in this obscure and therefore for him not entirely comprehensible death, decide concerning him.[179]

While it is true that man does not understand all that is entailed in his life after death, the obscurity here does not seem to be an ignorance of the complete nature of God, such as the mystics speak of, but rather a complete ignorance that one will find anything after death at all. "On the basis of human experience it is never possible to say whether death is really the true perfection or the true end of the man who has died."[180] Here one should note that end does not mean the goal of willed activity, but a complete passing away after the manner of the animals.

Rahner goes on to distinguish the human experience of death in the state of original justice and the state of original sin. For Adam, death was not hidden in darkness; he would have experienced death as personal consummation. But why? Only, it seems, because he could easily choose with the anticipation of Heidegger. Because Adam had divine grace, he easily surrendered himself in anguish to the possibility that God could surprise him.

The death of someone in sin, on the other hand, is very different. The absence of divine grace makes death empty. Strangely, though, Rahner thinks that death, which is a punishment for original sin, is mortal sin in the strictest sense of the word. Mortal sin, for him, would be identified with the very experience of physical death.

> Death is not only the expression and visible mark of man's alienation from God, of his lot since Adam's fall; it is also . . . a consequence of grave, personal (and unforgiven) sins.[181]

Death, then, in fallen man has two aspects. It expresses the opposition between body and spirit, and it seems totally in opposition to the fulfillment of spirit. On the other hand, death is merely material and cannot be reconciled with the interior life of man. It seems wholly violent. Both aspects of death must be affirmed;[182] the important thing in both is that one cannot possibly know what lies after death.

> It is not possible to say whether the full term of life reached in death is not in fact the emptiness and futility which till then was concealed, or, conversely, whether the emptiness apparent in death is only the outward aspect of a true plenitude, deceptive only to us who are not dead.[183]

How can any man make the most of death? Since he has no real knowledge of what the afterlife is like or, presumably, even if one exists, he must merely make the most of the possibilities. He does so through the life of faith. By it, man has an "unconditional openness to the disposition of the incomprehensible God, without presuming to know what that sovereign liberty of God may [...] decide concerning him."[184]

The most interesting application of this new theology of death relates to the death of Christ on the cross. At the beginning of his consideration of the death of Christ, Rahner summarizes what has gone before.

> [...] death is many-sided: action and suffering, a surrender of the bodily form and the opening out of a pancosmic relation of the spirit, an end of the historical life on a biological basis and the consummation of the personal life within.[185]

Rahner applies these various characteristics of death to the death of Christ. The key element in the death of Christ must be his "free acceptance of death."[186] This is the "moral work upon the performance of which God willed the restitution of grace to man to depend."[187] What does this mean?

Traditional Catholic theology affirms that the moral attitude of Christ, his sacrifice of self from obedience and love, is the key to understanding the redemptive nature of his death. However, this involves no ignorance of God or of his own destiny on the part of Christ. As both a comprehensor and a wayfarer, Christ knows the vision of God already in his human intellect and knows by a sort of infused or prophetic knowledge about his own resurrection, which he predicts many times. He therefore embraces death in no sense as a mere surrender to fate, but as a freely chosen act with *full prior knowledge of all the consequences.*

Without this knowledge, the moral freedom of his own death would be questionable because it would involve ignorance and compromise choice.

For Rahner, the moral will of Christ is very different. His sacrifice can only have value if it is like pagan man's. This means that Christ must experience the same obscurity of death as all the rest of mankind - not only mankind in general, but pagan mankind in particular, as will be evident later. One must remember that for Fr. Rahner, the very obscurity of death gives death its possibility.

Is this the life of faith? Rahner claims it is not. Still, if Christ knows more about what will happen to him than other men do, then he cannot experience the redemptive character of death. "Even though Christ was not in a state of belief, he nevertheless experienced in himself the darkness which is the specific character of human death and the deprivation of the personal consummation in the void of the bodily end."[188] Rahner is emphatic on this point. Christ could not have been perfectly obedient unto death unless he himself experienced darkness in death. "It is precisely in its darkness that the death of Christ becomes the expression and embodiment of his loving obedience."[189]

Christ could not have experienced this darkness if he enjoyed the Beatific Vision while he was on earth. This vision would have taken all of the emptying character out of death for Christ because he would have had some specific object to hope in besides the complete freedom and indefinability of God. Nor could Christ's descent into hell have occurred if he enjoyed the Beatific Vision, for Christ "[...] before his death, could not yet share in the vision of God."[190] Moreover, the death of Christ on the cross and the descent into hell allow him to establish an "open real ontological relationship to the world in its unity."[191]

By his death and descent into hell, Christ enters into the center of the whole world, so that the world is completely different in nature after his death than it was before; for "[...] the world as a whole and as the scene of personal life in the world has become different from what it would have been had Christ not died."[192] Not only this, but Christ becomes the whole universe in a material sense after his death because there is no longer any necessary relation between his soul and his individual body. "When the vessel of his body was shattered in death, Christ was poured out over all the cosmos; he became actually, in his very humanity, what he had always been in his dignity, the heart of the universe, the innermost centre of creation."[193]

Thus, Fr. Rahner and the many who follow his ideas specifically deny the possibility that the human soul of Christ enjoyed on earth the vision of God given to the blessed. This is precisely because Christ cannot experience *kenosis* (self-emptying) if he has possessed the vision of God. He cannot throw himself into the blackness of possibility and obscurity of death if he sees God in the face.[194]

In light of this theory, how is the Christian morally to confront his own death? Death is the saving event itself and, as Boros has maintained above, death is the one and unique final personal decision of one's life. The very emptiness of man in death allows God to fill it with his fullness. A Christian must face death in utter lack of knowledge and complete disinterest in what will come after. Man's experience of the very blackness of the alien world and his trust that God will somehow resolve this experience is the foundation of the redemptive character of the death of the Christian. "[...] [The] death itself of a man in the state of grace is a saving event. [...]death, as a human action, is precisely the event which gathers up the whole personal act of a human life into one fulfillment."[195]

The attitude of the Christian should imitate that of Christ, who gave himself completely into the obscure unknown with no real idea of how God would resolve a destructive situation. The Christian experiences existentially what seems like "remoteness from God"[196] and this remoteness is itself the "advent of God's plenitude"[197]. The very inability to understand what could possibly be in store for man after death forms the basis for the value of faith, hope and charity. Death involves the highest and most completely personal choice anyone ever makes. The value of death is the will to believe in spite of its existence. Christ's death

> as an act of grace, helped to offer to God the 'flesh of sin' - which death really is - transformed it into a flesh of grace; so that we now can, through his grace, belong to God and to Christ in death, despite the fact that death, in itself, means remoteness from God.[198]

> The trinity of faith, hope and charity makes death itself the highest act of believing, hoping, loving, the very death which seems to be absolute darkness, despair, coldness itself.[199]

In summary, Rahner's idea of death involves the following elements:

1. Death is the natural destiny of man as it is for the rest of creation.
2. Man is a being made for death. He must come to accept this fact in order to experience the fullness of what it means to be man.
3. The very darkness, absurdity and alienation of the material world from man, which are perfectly expressed in death, entail the possibility of transcending death. If man cannot know or suspect what lies beyond death or how God will resolve death, then he certainly cannot discount any solution God might offer to death.
4. Death then becomes possibility as Heidegger suggests, a doorway into something that could be wonderful. Man must convince himself of this, and this sustains him in the actual moment of death.

5. The attitude of man at the moment of death is decisive in his transcendence of death. If he finds no possibility there, death is merely a tragedy. If he finds an occasion in which he can fling himself into absurdity and darkness, knowing that God can do anything he wills with it, then he transcends it.
6. This kind of death was the death Christ died, a perfect image for Christian death. To look on death as possibility in darkness and to harrow hell, Christ could not have enjoyed the vision of God on the cross nor really have had any knowledge of the resurrection. He must have suffered just as much in darkness and alienation as any other man.
7. Death as an experience of complete absurdity and absolute freedom is itself a sacrament.

II. The True Nature of Death

The modern position on death inspired by Heideggerian philosophy is patently anti-Christian. It is also patently against reason. Reason defines the natural character of death; faith defines death as a punishment for original sin. In both cases, death is more than simply a possibility for the remedy of a psychologically perceived absurdity.

The most vital question in any study of the nature of death is just exactly in what sense death can be said to be the destiny of man. This will help to answer the further question of the natural character of death. St. Thomas is very clear about the nature of death. "The necessity of dying for man is partly from nature and partly from sin."[200]

The fact that death is due to nature is caused by the contrary elements in the body. Every material body is composed of both active and passive elements, held together in a tenuous connection. From the point of view of these elements, death is natural, nor is there any power in the material elements themselves or in the soul to keep the body from death. Considered from the point of view of the body, then, man is mortal and doomed to die.

Yet man is not only a body, but also a soul. The soul is the spiritual element in man's composition, the form of the body, and the element that organizes matter into the being which is man. Body and soul are not two separate principles, but complementary ones that must exist in union with each other for man to exist perfectly. Soul, or form exists within matter, and organizes it because man is not an angel. Body could not exist as human without soul. Thus, the destiny of man could in no sense be determined by only one of the elements; it requires both. Though the body tends to death because of its contrary elements, it tends to life because of the presence of the soul.

In fact, from the point of view of the soul, death is not natural to man.

> A thing is said to be natural if it proceeds from the principles of nature. Now the essential principles of nature are form and matter. The form of man is his rational soul, which is immortal: wherefore death is not natural to man on the part of his form.[201]

Though it is true that, naturally speaking, death is the destiny of man (if one considers man only from the point of view of the body), nothing could be further from the truth if one considers man from the point of view of the form which is the spiritual soul.

Reason can consider the destiny of the soul and realize that there is an act of man, intelligence, that goes beyond the act of the body and is not open to death. Some ancient philosophers knew this. According to St. Thomas, for example, Aristotle maintained the soul was immortal from reason alone.

> This conclusion also comes to light through the authority of Aristotle. For he says in De Anima, I, 4 (408b 18) that *the intellect is evidently a substance and is incapable of being destroyed.*[202]

The first implication this idea should have for the discussion of death is that it is absolutely impossible, even from the standpoint of reason, to maintain that death is the final destiny of man considered as a whole, or that life for that reason is absurd. Death is a fact, but it cannot be the destiny of man, for this would reduce man to only the material order. This position was maintained by many of the ancients; St. Thomas, quoting Seneca, observes, "Death is of the nature of man, not a punishment."[203] But death is only natural to man from the point of view of matter. In fact, if man is a composition of matter and form, and the soul is immortal, then, logically speaking, the whole man should live forever. In fact, this is the way things ought to be. Yet all know that it is not.

There is no solution to the problem of death until human destiny is considered from the point of view of the soul. St. Thomas makes the point many times that the soul in its act can only be fulfilled in the act of the intellect. Once the intellect knows one relation of cause and effect, then the power of the mind cannot be stilled until the first cause is directly experienced. Aristotle speaks of this intellectual dynamism in the first book of his Metaphysics.

> For it is owing to their wonder that men both now begin and at first began to philosophize; they wondered originally at the obvious difficulties, then advanced little by little and stated difficulties about greater matters [...] for we say we know each thing only when we recognize its first cause.[204]

St. Thomas makes much of this text when he discusses the problem of human destiny, as we have seen in Chapter One. He reproduces it almost exactly when he considers that even reason can reach the necessary conclusion that man must see God to be fulfilled. This is because of the natural desire of the intellect. If this is true, then man must be able to live forever.

> Therefore some who considered this, held that no created intellect could see the essence of God. [...] Further the same opinion is also against reason. For these resides in every man a natural desire to know the cause of any effect which he sees; and thence arises wonder in man. But if the intellect of the rational creature could not reach so far as to the first cause of things, the natural desire would remain void.[205]

St. Thomas invokes the same text in several arguments, to show that neither angels nor men could find their happiness and their destiny consisting in anything less than the vision of God.[206] This truth is one that St. Thomas cites in that section of the Summa Contra Gentiles which contains truths accessible to demonstrative arguments from reason alone. This leads one to conclude that though, by nature, the body has only death as its lot, by nature the soul can only have God for its lot. "As the soul is the life of the body, so God is the happy life of man."[207]

If the vision of God is the fulfillment of the soul and the soul is the life of the body, then by implication death cannot be man's end. Moreover, the body really ought not to die in perpetuity. A philosopher would have to conclude that though the body does die, the soul lives forever, and that this is not a natural condition, because the perpetual division of the dead body and the immortally living soul would be a violent condition. According to Aristotle, anti-natural or violent conditions cannot exist in perpetuity.[208]

Therefore these considerations led ancient thinkers to a philosophical box canyon.[209] Man considered in this way was truly an absurdity.

The solution to this problem can only be resurrection, but there is no power on earth that can bring about resurrection. We are left with the absurdity that the body lies dead forever while the soul lives forever - the absurdity the ancient philosophers were led to when they tried to resolve this contradiction by reason alone. In fact, the resolution is not possible by reason alone. One must know revelation, and especially the fact of the resurrection, to resolve it.

Actually, the ancient philosophers could not have resolved this problem because they did not know that man had been or could be called to intimacy with God. Though they knew that nothing in this world could be the complete life of the soul, and that the body should not die, they had no idea how either of these facts which they experienced could be explained. They took the nature they experienced to be nature as it ought to be. It was, in fact, fallen nature, but they did not know this. Seneca said death was the nature of man because he did not know the Scriptures, nor did he know about the condition of man before the Fall.

> Seneca and the other philosophers considered human nature according to those things which belong to it from the principles of nature: for they did not know about that state of the first condition, which is only held by faith; and therefore they only spoke about death as about a natural defect, although a natural defect can be a punishment in some way.[210]

The nature of man was created correctly by God in the beginning. So, in order to understand fully the mystery of death, one must first examine human nature as it came originally from the hands of God. Since man is made for

God, God in his infinite goodness (from the supposition of his having created a reasoning creature) provided for his fulfillment. God created man in grace, without sin. Grace resided in the very essence of the soul and by it man was made capable of communion with God. Grace most fittingly should be received in a human character that is created whole.

This wholeness had to include the body as well as the soul because man is the composite of both. God therefore most fittingly instilled in human nature a state in which all of the powers of the human soul were one with the supernatural orientation of the soul. The body was created in fit service to such a marvelous and right union, and God exteriorly preserved it from death. The gifts given to both soul and body are called the preternatural gifts (the Latin word <u>praeter</u> means "beyond" but not "above"); exterior protection from death is among them. Habitual union with God is above nature; the gifts of the integrity of body and the powers of the soul are not. They are beyond nature, but strictly speaking are not supernatural, for they do not involve unity with the Trinity as such. They are, however, caused by the supernatural gift of grace.

Man was not in any sense born to die, then, as he came from the hands of the Creator. In his original creation, Adam had grace in the soul and a gift by which his body was preserved from death. Yet this gift was not so intrinsic to the body that the body was identified with the resurrected body. Adam still had to eat to maintain his life; the propagation of the race still depended on conjugal sexual activity.

In other words, the condition of unity and integrity of the human character was only as permanent as the state of grace. God subjected man to a beautiful union of love in which divine love and life permeated all of the powers of man, but this condition could in no sense be controlled by human power. Man could in no sense preserve himself in this marvelous unity; he had continually to rely on the hand of the loving God to sustain him in such a condition. This reliance was on actual grace. Because he had to motivate every act by the divine intimacy and with the divine support, this condition endured as long as man continued to return all that was his to God in loving communion. In short, it endured as long as man obeyed God's law.

> But nevertheless in the state of innocence a kind of gift had been internally given freely by God to the soul, that outside the order of other forms it might bestow a life without defect on the body according to its own manner. As the soul is not corruptible, the body might remain altogether subject to the soul not according to the manner of a corruptible body for as long as the soul remained subject to God. Nor could a disposition occur in the body which could impede the life-giving ability of the soul.[211]

After sin, the soul of man lost grace. Since union with grace was the source of the marvelous union of all the powers of human nature, the loss of grace left man's nature to those devices which nature possessed on it own. There is no natural power in the soul or body to keep the body alive forever, and so the necessity of death entered the world.

> But after sin this gift was lost, and therefore human nature was left [...] in a state which was due to it from the power of its own principles according to which it is said to it (Gen. 3:19): 'You are dust and to dust you shall return.'
>
> Therefore after sin, the necessity of dying entered man from sin, as removing something which prohibits the grace of innocence; but also from the nature of matter because from it per se comes the necessity of death.[212]

Man would have had to die had he not been created in grace. Given the fact that he was created in grace, and that creation in grace was central to the fulfillment of human nature and due to divine goodness, death is a punishment "by comparison to the state of innocence."[213]

After the Fall, man could only be aware of those powers which were open to him according to the potencies in his soul and body. This was not a "natural" state, however. It was, rather, "fallen nature". Grace and divine communion are so central to the fulfillment of human nature that human nature without it lives in an impaired state.

There are, then, two deaths in man in the state of original sin. Sin, the death of the soul, is the cause of the necessary death of the body. Of course, the soul does not die ontologically. By nature, the soul lives forever. However, the soul without grace is described as dead because God is its life. Without the supporting aid of communion with God, then, death of the body is a natural consequence.

> Man has a twofold death and a twofold life. The first death is the death of the body, brought about by separation from the soul; the second death is brought about by the separation of the soul from God. [...] Similarly, opposed to this twofold death we are to understand there is a twofold life. One is a life of the body imparted by the soul, and this is called the life of nature. The other comes from God and is called the life of justice or the life of grace.[214]

By way of conclusion, it is obvious that far from a flight into fanciful possibility, the death of man is a tragedy that is caused by a much deeper tragedy, the death brought by sin. The experience of death without knowing about grace causes an extreme tension within each human person, because death seems so unnatural and absurd. This is not because life after death is just some sort of wishful thinking. The necessity of the afterlife is perfectly reasonable.

But man in the state of sin is left in a box canyon without an exit.[215] This is because man can know that the soul lives forever. However, for the body not to share in this life is a violence man cannot explain. The source of the tragedy is sin, of course; but though the philosopher who relies only on reason can recognize this as an intolerable condition, he cannot possibly know why it exists.

The problem is not that man is hopeless and finds life completely absurd, something of which he can make no sense. Rather, the source of the absurdity is that man knows that his life is eternal, but, in the first place, because of the "death of the soul" he has no power to arrive at any object that is eternal. Secondly, even if he could, his body cannot follow where his soul would lead. If one were a Platonist, this would pose no problem. But for one who understands both the eternity of the soul and the substantial unity of body and soul, the death of the body is a double absurdity *because of the immortality of the soul.*

But nihilism and existential anguish have no place here. If death were man's destiny, sin would not be madness. However, the madness of sin comes from the fact that man will exist, but in a completely unfulfilled state. Man without grace can have no natural completion, and there can be no completion for the eternally existing soul because union with God is impossible. If one knows his soul is immortal yet cannot know that union with God is possible, this is the most unhappy of worlds. There can be no completion of the body because there is no power in the soul or the body to make it live forever with the soul.

All then becomes violence. The soul without the possibility of communion with God experiences a violence of nature. The body without possibility of eternal union with the soul experiences the same.

But grace changes all this. The person who understands the possibility of salvation understands that there is a remedy for the death of soul that allows one again to arrive at communion with God. The person who knows revelation also understands that the cause of the corruption of death is the loss of grace to the soul. Nevertheless, death would still be problematic had Christ not risen from the dead.

When Christ rose from the dead, he established the perfect complement to the life of grace he gave to the soul in his death, for redemption would not be complete without the resurrection. A two-fold life corresponds to the two-fold death: "Accordingly, resurrection is also twofold: one is a bodily resurrection, in which the soul is united to the body for the second time; the other is a spiritual resurrection, in which the soul is again united to God."[216]

Man's true existential angst can only be over the existence of sin. Such uneasiness is found in pagans who do not know that their nature is not as nature ought to be. Man can also be uneasy if he knows about grace, but cannot arrive at heaven because of sin. It would contradict both reason and faith to maintain that man is uneasy at existence because he finds only darkness and nothingness when he thinks about the possibility of death; reason teaches, and faith confirms, that the soul lives forever. However, the death of the body is problematic, and the very difficulty is caused <u>because</u> man knows he can live forever and his actions influence his destiny.

Chapter 7
ATTITUDES TO DEATH

I. Application to the Death of Christ

Perhaps no theological problem in the Church has caused more difficulty than the death of Christ. On this question depends the whole idea of the life and nature of Christ. Since Christ is the very Image of the Father, in both his divine and his human nature, all Christian anthropology is decided in relation to his person. This, of course, includes the question of the end of man and therefore the structure of the soul. Christ is, in every sense of the words, "man fully alive".

This problem is further related to the problem of the human knowledge of Christ. For example, it is common today to maintain as Rahner does (against all the tradition of the faith) that Jesus did not enjoy the Beatific Vision until after the Resurrection.[217] It is argued that the presence of the Beatific Vision on the cross would not allow Christ to experience the true angst of human death, nor permit him to enter completely into the human drama. Such knowledge would both limit his atonement, because it would limit his experience of the darkness which each man must experience, and reduce his trust in God, because it would give some real positive content and satisfaction to his hope instead of testifying to his trust in God in the face of existential fear.

> As Christ became man of the fallen race of Adam, and assumed the 'flesh of sin', he entered human life in a situation in which that life reaches its fulfilment [sic] only by passing through death in all its obscurity. That is, he took death upon himself inasmuch as in the actual order of things it is an expression and manifestation of the fallen state of creation in

> both angels and in man. Even though Christ was not in a state of belief, he nevertheless experienced in himself the darkness which is the specific character of human death and the deprivation of the personal consummation in the void of the bodily end.[218]

The kenosis or emptying of Christ, thus, must have been an emptying of all real and intimate knowledge of his Father. Had he known God, he could certainly not have been in a void. Holy Christians often seem to themselves to be in a void at death, but this is due to their love running ahead of their knowledge. For Rahner, following Heidegger, this very void is the natural condition of man. For the whole modern school, a man who is not ignorant, who is not disordered in his passions, or who cannot be internally tempted is not human, nor is a man who does not have anguish over darkness in death. For many modern theologians, to seek a reasonable explanation for the cry of Christ from the cross, "My God, My God, why have you forsaken me?" is not only a futile, but also an inhuman exercise. Christ experienced the same darkness in faith that we experience and that is that.

Yet, as has been demonstrated, the nature of man does not demand that one affirm that death is mere possibility or existential angst. The darkness of death is not due to the fact that it is a total void. To say so would be the complete denial of metaphysics in the order of nature.

Not only does Jesus' enlightenment with the Beatific Vision not detract from his humanity, it places his humanity in the proper attitude towards suffering. For any reasoning man, and even more for the believing Christian, death cannot be a thrust into the void of possibility, like the Götterdämerung of pagan German philosophy of the 19th century. Suffering is tolerated in light of hope held in store for us by the knowledge of faith, a true knowledge with concepts and conclusions. For Christ, who could not have had faith (otherwise he would have been only an adopted son), human knowledge of the vision of God while on earth only showed what the true end of man is. Does this lessen the pain of his death? Not in the least! It rather adds to it. With lightening-swift speed of mind, Christ appreciated more than any other human being the gulf between sin, which destroyed his body, and God, whose vision he enjoyed while this was happening. Most traditional theologians teach that without the knowledge of the vision and certainty of resurrection, Christ could not have sustained the obedience of the passion.

Pope Pius XII spoke of the necessity of this knowledge of the Beatific Vision in Mystici Corporis:

> The loving knowledge with which the divine Redeemer has pursued us from the first moment of his Incarnation is such as completely to surpass the searchings of the human mind; for by means of the beatific vision, *which he enjoyed from the time when he was received into the womb of the Mother of God,* he has forever and continuously had present to him all the members of his mystical body, and embraced them with his saving love. [...] In the manger, on the cross, in the eternal glory of the Father, Christ sees and embraces all the members of his Church, and he sees them far more clearly, embraces them far more lovingly, than does a mother the child of her bosom, far better than a man knows and loves himself.[219]

The same doctrine is taught in the Catechism of the Catholic Church. "But at the same time, this truly human knowledge of God's Son expressed the divine life of his person. [...] Such is the case first of all with the intimate and immediate knowledge that the Son of God made man had of his Father."[220]

The death of Christ, then, which is the model for all Christian attitudes towards death, was not a surrender to the void of fate with some desperate velleity that something wonderful he could not foresee might come out of this tragedy. Rather, it was a voluntary human act. Christ could have willed not to die had he so wished. Rather, He embraced death, not as the end or purpose of human life (which is the vision of God), but so that he might take his life up again by his own free will.[221] He embraced death to take upon himself the punishment for our sin.

His cry from the cross, then - "My God, My God, why have you forsaken me?" - is hardly a cry of despair in the midst of untold agony. Most traditional exegetes understand this cry as the first words of a Psalm which probably Christ recited in its entirety *sotto voce.* The Psalm does express deep anguish in suffering, but it is not anguish in a void. It ends in confident assurance that God has and will vindicate his suffering servant.[222]

The anguish and emptiness that Jesus experiences exist only in his feelings, on the level of his senses. In his intellect and will, Jesus is always in the presence of God through the Beatific Vision.

> Jesus had the clear vision of God and the certainty of his union with the Father dominant in his mind. But in the sphere bordering on the senses, and therefore subject to the impressions, emotions and influences of the internal and external experiences of pain, Jesus' human soul was reduced to a wasteland.[223]

In speaking of Christ's death and <u>kenosis,</u> one must ask how the death occurred and what exactly was the emptying, for the pattern of Christ's death will be a model for the attitude of all Christians towards their own death. Christ could have emptied himself in five ways.[224] He could have abandoned the union of the Word with the Father within the Trinity. This was impossible. He could have abandoned his own union of his divine personhood with human nature by the hypostatic union. This was also impossible. He could have abandoned the union that he had by human nature with grace, and become a sinner, but this would in no way have contributed to the purpose of the Incarnation, to reverse the disobedience of sin. Finally, he could have abandoned the vision of God - he would have to possess it to abandon it—but once possessed the vision is so compelling that it cannot be lost.

The abandonment can therefore be on none of these levels, for any one would detract from the mystery of Christ's Person or the mystery of the atonement, or would simply not be fitting to him. The only level on which Christ can be abandoned, then, is that of the *union of protection*.[225] Christ was in no sense desolate in his higher soul, puzzled at the reason for his death, or uncertain of the ultimate victory of the resurrection. He suffered all knowingly so that his obedience could be perfect. Christ was abandoned only in being externally delivered to "the power of his persecutor and feeling this;"[226] God in no sense abandoned his soul. Indeed, Christ sent forth the Spirit in which he was conceived by his own power, in the loud cry from the Cross. "It was the peculiar privilege of Christ the Lord to have died when he himself decreed to die, and to have died not so much by external violence as by internal assent. Not only his death, but also its time and place, were ordained by him."[227]He felt abandoned and in agony because of the pain in his body and the rejection of all men. This feeling did not arrive at his higher self.

The idea of death in Christianity has nothing whatever to do with the idea of death in Heidegger. In fact, the two are diametrically opposed because they are based on two diametrically opposed metaphysics. Fr. Bertrand de Margerie states this opposition well in his work on the exegesis of St. Augustine.

> This (feeling forsaken) is a theme which impresses us all the more today, since Heidegger's theme of dereliction (*Geworfenheit*) has spread far and wide: man thrown into a hostile, overwhelming and threatening world, feels abandoned by it. [...]It should be noted, however, that the similarity is only superficial. Augustine's world is not essentially inimical to man, for it is the world of the provident God, who is the Creator. Contrary to Heidegger's view, our presence in the world is neither absurd not without reason.[228]

The idea of death in the work of modern theologians is not only untenable, but also based on a worldview completely contrary to both reason and faith. Reason demonstrates that the vision of God is the only thing that can quiet man's intellect, and therefore man must be ordered to that vision by nature. Death can in no sense be the end of human nature. Rather, the existence of death poses a great problem for reason because of the union of the soul. The existence of death poses no problem for sense knowledge because it is a fact and there is no power in the body or the soul to keep the body living forever. Yet, death as an everlasting condition is an absurdity because of the spirituality of the soul.

As to faith, the real death is not the death of the body, but the death of the soul caused by sin. There are no compelling reasons to maintain that Christ experienced any sort of death of soul except in his passions. In fact, to maintain this would contradict both the nature of the Incarnation and its purpose, the atonement for the disobedience of the original sin by the perfect obedience of Christ. Moreover, the denial of the vision of God, the destiny of human nature, to the soul of Christ while on earth makes no sense either. Christ would have had to merit it by his death for himself, which also unseats the perfect love of the Incarnation. Even if Christ had not enjoyed such a vision, to maintain that he knew nothing about it or about his resurrection makes him less than what tradition has always ascribed to Adam before the fall and to the holy Christian after a graced life. Life is not a hostile void except in the eyes of those who live by an imperfect metaphysics.

II. The Christian Attitude towards Death

What, then, should be the attitude of the Christian in the face of death? Obviously, it should be the same as our Lord's. For the Christian, death is not a darkness, an absurdity, nor a plunge into a nonsensical unknown. The Christian knows death is painful and sorrowful. It is not a pleasant experience; it is a punishment for original sin.

Still, the Christian should not worry about physical death. What gives death its sting is not the fact that the body loses life and corrupts in the grave. One who has lived a life of union with God on earth knows with the firmest conviction of faith that the soul lives forever. One also knows, following the resurrection of Christ, that he will have a part in that resurrection. The real problem with death is that it is painful. For one who has faith there should be no uncertainty about what lies beyond death, nor should one have to resolve the seeming contradiction of a spirit's dying by merely "projecting" something after death. The real absurdity in death consists in someone's knowing what lies beyond the grave and yet going to it unprepared. Sin is the absurdity. In other words, the tragedy of death consists in experiencing the death of the body while one is experiencing the death of soul from sin. "O death, where is thy victory? O death, where is thy sting? The sting of death is sin, and the power of sin is the law."[229]

Rahner might answer that preparation for death demands that the will make sense of the absurd. But how could will change fact? Unless one has experienced the presence of the living God throughout life, wishful thinking will not resolve the unknown. God is not unknown to the soul in the state of grace. It is true one does not know him as well on earth as one will in heaven, but one knows him, nonetheless, and this knowledge of faith, especially if enlivened by love, is already a foretaste of heaven.

> Faith makes us taste in advance the light of the beatific vision, the goal of our journey here below. Then we shall see God 'face to face,' 'as he is'. So faith is already the beginning of eternal life.[230]

In baptism the Christian has already put to death the power of physical death, by being plunged into the mystery of Christ's death and resurrection. As the Christian begins to participate in the life of the Holy Spirit through baptism, his interior life is already experiencing intimacy with God, and the only real death which is a trial for the Christian now is the mystical death in struggling with sin. The engraced person grows more and more in appreciating the divine point of view, and this is painful, because the divine is not a point of view open to the normal discourse and love of men. Through grace, the inner life of the Trinity in eternity becomes the central human experience of everyday life. The death of the spirit to all that is not God is the source of human suffering. "These are the ones who suffer with impatient love, for they cannot remain long without either receiving or dying."[231]

All of a Christian's life is a preparation for heaven by a union of love, a heaven which is experienced in both body and soul. The acts of each and every day, thus, may be more important in manifesting a lifelong love and choice of heaven than any choice made at the moment of death, although conversion in articulo mortis is always possible and accepted by God. Still, this does not mean that the last moment of life is necessarily the most important. In fact, many are not conscious in their last moments. An individual may make many more important choices throughout his life, each one of which may merit heaven, otherwise grace would be ineffective.

It makes no sense at all to maintain that this one final choice, which is the only "real" one, must occur at the time the soul is separated from the body and yet does not experience metaphysical death. This would be to unseat every statement in philosophy and scripture that claims that each and every human act is preparatory for either heaven or hell. Those preparatory acts must be made in union with the body. Indeed, each ordinary act is the place where the life of the spirit is intensified.

> God still speaks as he spoke to our Fathers, when there were neither spiritual directors nor set methods. Then they saw that each moment brings with it a duty to be faithfully fulfilled. That was enough for spiritual perfection. On that duty their whole attention was fixed at each successive moment like the hand of a clock which marks the hours. Under the continuous impulse of God, their spirit found itself turning to each new object as it was presented to them by God at each hour of the day.[232]

The whole attempt to reduce the Christian experience of union with God to one ultimate final choice in the face of absurdity is completely contrary to everything true metaphysics and Catholic theology teach. The idea of death which it proposes as Christian is not even good paganism, for even intelligent pagans knew there was an eternal world which was filled with light and not darkness. Plato wrongly thought that the soul had existed in this world prior to its union with the flesh, but this was because, for Plato, intellectual knowledge involved no union with the flesh. Aristotle knew that the intellect as a power is ordered to knowing the First Cause itself, which can be nothing but an immaterial and eternal being. This can only be known by an immaterial and eternal light, but gained through the senses.

The life of the Christian must be a daily death to sin. Many mystical authors attest to this, taking their basis from St. Paul.

> What a going out from self that implies! What a death! Let us say with St. Paul, 'Quotidie morior (I die daily).' The great saint wrote to the Colossians, 'You have died and your life is hidden with Christ in God.'

That is the condition: we must be dead! Without that we may be hidden in God at certain moments; but we do not LIVE habitually in this divine Being because all our emotions, self-seeking and the rest, come to draw us out of Him.[233]

If the day of death were the only completely personal act which a person made, that day would mark the only merit of his final perseverance. In fact, each day opportunities are offered to the Christian by which he is invited to die to self. Those acts are often much more personal than acts performed in the "moment of death" and each one is sufficient to merit heaven.

> Some have said that no one *absolutely* merits life everlasting except by the act of final grace, but only *conditionally*, i.e. if he preservers. But it is unreasonable to say this, for sometimes the act of the last grace is not more, but less meritorious than preceding acts, on account of the prostration of illness. Hence it must be said that every act of charity merits eternal life absolutely [...][234]

The day of death is very important for the Christian, but for most it is not the day of the greatest act of perseverance nor of free choice. There can be no state after death, or in some no-man's-land between death and eternity, in which a person makes his only really personal act, because by then he is free from his body. Man can merit nothing without the body; every act of charity he performs in the body roots him in unity with the Trinity, his final home. The day of death is that day of final birth into eternal life, a life which has been continually nurtured by every human choice here on earth.

> For the Christian the day of death inaugurates, *at the end of his sacramental life*, the fulfillment of his new birth begun at Baptism, the definitive "conformity" to "the image of the Son" conferred by the anointing of the Holy Spirit, and participation in the feast of the Kingdom which was anticipated in the Eucharist.[235]

Chapter 8
BREAD OF ANGELS AND FOOD OF PILGRIMS: THE MYSTERY OF TRANSUBSTANTIATION

In his celebrated biography of the life of Thomas Aquinas, Fr. James Weisheipl describes St. Thomas' last communion in this way.

> Abbot Theobald brought the Eucharist to him. Before receiving Communion, Thomas said in the presence of the 'whole community of monks and many Dominicans and Friars Minor' many 'beautiful things' concerning his firm belief in the real presence, and in particular this: 'I have taught and written much on this most holy Body and on the other sacraments, according to my faith in Christ and in the holy Roman church, to whose judgement I submit all my teaching.'[236]

Man's pilgrimage as an image of God towards heaven is supported and sustained by the body and blood of Christ. No theology of "man fully alive" could be complete without an examination of the doctrine of the Holy Eucharist. This doctrine has a long history, and it has always existed amid theological controversy. The nature of the true change in the body and blood of Christ is a further application of the theme of this book, which examines man's relation to the supernatural order and various analogical and real aspects of the distinction between form and matter or body and soul as they contribute to man's realizing his final destiny.

"Ave verum corpus natum de Maria Virgine." "Hail, true *body* born from the Virgin Mary." Catholics have sung these beloved words through the ages in every musical setting, from Gregorian chant to Mozart. They express a theme first explicitly taught around 830 by a Benedictine monk, Paschasius Radbert (c.790-865), in a treatise he produced to explain the faith of the Catholic church about the Holy Eucharist, De Corpore et Sanguine Domini. In this treatise, Paschasius taught that the relation of the Body and Blood of Christ in the Eucharist and that of the Body and Blood of Christ born of the Virgin Mary is not merely "one of continuity but of essential sameness."[237]

This work initiated a long dispute on the nature of the presence of Christ in the Eucharist. Some thought that it was so real that when one ate the host one was actually crushing the body of Christ in heaven. This was the ultra-realist position. Included in this idea was the notion that the bleeding of the Host when it was broken, as in the miracle of Bolsena, was the normal manifestation of the Real Presence.

Others thought that the change was merely in sign, or in the meaning which the bread and wine took on in the context of the Eucharist. The principal proponent of this position was the French priest Berengar (c.1010-1088). He seems to have vacillated in his idea of the Eucharist between the idea that there was a real presence of Christ without true conversion of the elements into the body and blood of Christ (later Luther's position) and a more radical denial of the Real Presence at all, in which he claimed that the consecrated bread and wine merely *mean* Christ (later the position of Zwingli).[238]

In response to the difficulties caused by the extreme realism and extreme idealism of these positions, Lanfranc of Bec sought to clarify the doctrine of the church on this subject. He did so using Aristotelian philosophy.

> The material objects on the Lord's Table which God sanctifies through the priest are, by the agency of God's power, indefinably, wondrously, in a way beyond our understanding, converted to the body of Christ in their being. *Their outward appearances and*

> *certain other qualities remain unchanged*, so that those who receive them are not shocked by the naked flesh and blood, and so that believers may receive the greater rewards of faith. What we receive is the very body which was born of the Virgin, and yet it is not. It is, in respect to its being (*essentia*) and the characteristics and power of its true nature; it is not if you look at the outward appearances (*species*) of the bread and wine.[239]

This solution led to the final definition of the Fourth Lateran Council in 1215 concerning the manner in which Christ is present in the sacrament of the Eucharist.

> There is one universal Church of the faithful, outside which, no one at all is in a state of salvation. In this Church, Jesus Christ himself is both priest and sacrifice; and his body and blood are really contained in the sacrament of the altar under the species of bread and wine, the bread being transubstantiated into the body and the wine into the blood, by the power of God, so that, to effect the mystery of unity, we ourselves receive of that which is his, what he himself received of that which is ours.[240]

The Fourth Lateran Council used the word "transubstantiation" to summarize a long tradition originating in the Gospels and St. Paul concerning the presence of Christ in the Eucharist. This term is a rich mine from which all sorts of further reflections on the theology of the Eucharist have developed. We shall examine them now and use them to meditate on the beautiful sequence composed by Thomas Aquinas for the Mass of Corpus Christi, <u>Lauda Zion Salvatorem</u>.

First, one must understand what the term "transubstantiation" means: that after the priest says the words of institution over the bread, the being of bread is changed into the being (essential or physical nature, what it is) of the body of Christ, but all the properties (external appearances) of bread remain. In the late 60's I attended a lecture by a Catholic priest-theologian given to a large group of Protestant and Catholic seminarians in Berkeley, California, in which he declared that, according to the doctrine of transubstantiation, if one put the consecrated host under a microscope, he would see the molecules of Christ's body. As medieval theologians had no access to microscopes, they could not know that this was not true. However, modern scientific investigation had demonstrated that since there was no change in molecular structure, there was no change in substance. As a result, the priest claimed, modern science demonstrated that the change must be a change not in being, but only in being perceived by the subject through his faith and in the use the subject makes of the consecrated bread. In other words, the bread now means Christ to the subject and he uses it for the purpose of union with Christ. (These last ideas are generally termed "transignification" [change in meaning] and "transfinalization" [change in purpose].)

The difficulties in this position are, first, that it mistakes the classical notion of "substance" for the modern idea of chemical-molecular composition. Substance in the philosophical sense does not refer to elements, but to a being which exists in its own right. A dog is a substance, as is a man, bread, or a rock. Also, an "accident" is not an unforeseen event, but a being which cannot exist in its own right. The color white is an accident, because white cannot exist apart from a white thing, like a white dog, a white man, white bread or a white rock. Transubstantiation does not mean that molecular structure changes, for such a change is merely an accidental expression of the material quantity of the substance.

Second, while it is true to say that the change that occurs in the Eucharist includes change in meaning and change in purpose, this is precisely because it involves change in nature. In other words, the objective change must support the subjective change, otherwise, the Eucharist would merely involve a change in sign, not in truth. Pope Paul VI expresses this very well.

> As a result of transubstantiation, the species of bread and wine undoubtedly take on a new meaning and a new finality, for they no longer remain ordinary bread and ordinary wine, but become the sign of something sacred, the sign of a spiritual food. However, the reason why they take on this new significance and this new finality is because they contain a new reality which we justly term "ontological". For there no longer lies under those species what was there before, but something quite different; and that, not only because of the faith of the Church, but in objective reality.[241]

Christ came in this new way to give the gift of himself to the Church. Though one can only know this new way, this change, by faith, it is not just a change in human knowledge with no relation to the reality of the bread itself. Our Lord gave us this gift to perfect our union with him. Christ began this union by associating the twelve apostles with him in his future passion at the Last Supper.

> Laud,O Zion, your salvation
> Laud with hymns of exultation
> Christ, your king and shepherd true;
> Bring him all the praise you know,
> He is more than you bestow
> Never can you reach his due.

Special theme for glad thanksgiving
Is the quick'ning and the living
Bread today before you set:
From his hands of old partaken,
As we know by faith unshaken,
Where the Twelve at supper met.

He completes this union by associating us with his passion, suffered and accepted, and with his body, resurrected and ascended. The new and eternal Covenant must be more perfect than the Old Covenant, which only sacrificed Christ in sign. Sign generally refers to something which represents something other than itself to man. Since man is a reasoning being, it is possible for him to relate one thing to something completely different through knowledge. The Paschal Lamb, for instance, represents something other than itself, Christ. If the change in the Eucharist were only of this character, it would only be bread which we would understand to be Christ. The change would be only in our minds, not in the reality of the bread.

The New Law must contain the accepted sacrifice of Christ in very truth, for atonement demands both resolution of disobedience (sacrifice of will through suffering some defect of original sin) and imparting of interior union with God (grace). Every Christian must constantly be nourished by the continuous spiritual and physical presence of Christ to interiorly avoid sin and live the life of grace. This can only happen if Christ becomes truly present to us here on earth so that we may participate in his body and blood and make his perfectly obedient soul our own. Christ loves us and wants to be completely with us on our journey of faith.

The Eucharist is the bond of love and stimulus for hope, because in this food we become the food, whereas in all other cases the food becomes us. In sharing the Eucharist we are more and more transformed into Christ. Still, because we only know him here through faith, this sacrament is also a food for our faith by which the interior obedience and love of

Christ's human heart become the constant nourishment for our spirits. Thus, the Eucharist is the food of pilgrims.

Full and clear ring out your chanting,
joy nor sweetest grace be wanting,
From your heart let praises burst:
For today the feast is holden
When the institution olden
Of that supper was rehearsed.

Here the new law's new oblation
By the new king's revelation,
Ends the form of ancient rite:
Now the new the old effaces,
Truth away the shadow chases,
Light dispels the gloom of night.

Christ wishes to be intimately present to everyone in his true body and blood. He could not do this if he were only present as his body is present in heaven. The Blessed Sacrament is truly that body, but it is present in a substantial, sacramental way. His body does not move through space to leave heaven and become present; first on one altar on earth, then on another. The change of transubstantiation is not a change in shape or a change in place, depth, height or density; it is a true change in substance. The dimensions and quantity of Christ's risen body remain at the right hand of the Father, which becomes completely present on all the altars of the world, completely and simultaneously, otherwise we would not all participate equally in the fullness of his obedience and love. The quantity of Christ's body is an accident. This accident extends a subject into parts. These parts may be either number, as in 1, 2, 3, 4 apples or magnitude, length and depth, as in one apple which is larger than another. Christ's risen body *is* present in the Eucharist, but not as an accident. It is present there because the substance is present.

The change in the Eucharist is like no other change in nature. The sacrament is a sign of Christ's body and blood in the sense that the body and blood become present in the manner of a sacrament. All that we need to perceive the value of the sign is for the appearances that we know with the five senses to remain for us. But this sacrament is more than a sign. Not only is the form of the being changed, but the normal vehicle of the change (the matter) does not endure. This means that the change of transubstantiation is unlike any other natural change, for in all other natural changes, there is a medium which must remain, while the properties express the change from one thing to another in the underlying medium. For example, in sculpting the block of marble, the marble is the medium that changes from a block to a statue. The properties would be the height, depth, shape, etc. of the marble. When a living body changes to a dead body, the primary matter of the living body is the subject that survives as the primary matter of the dead body. This is a change in substance and the primary matter is the potential to change which deeply underlies all beings. Matter is the vehicle of change; form and properties are the things that change. Since the soul has left the body, the body becomes cold and stiff. The heart ceases to beat. These are the properties of a dead body as opposed to a living one.

In the Eucharist, on the other hand, the whole substance, both form and primary matter, are instantaneously converted into the body of Christ, yet the appearances or properties of bread miraculously remain. The bread still looks, tastes and feels like bread. It still gets stale after a period of time. Its molecular structure still remains. These appearances are not an illusion; they are truly what the senses perceive and they truly express the thing that is there. They do what is characteristic of properties. But they do so by miraculous conservation because they do not inhere in the being of the body of Christ. In all other changes, other properties inhere in the new being. The *appearances* of the precious blood would make someone drunk if he drank too much; the *appearances* of bread would nourish, if enough were eaten. Yet what happens to them does not happen to the substance of the body of Christ. If they are divided, the body of Christ is not divided in heaven. If they are moved, the body of Christ is not moved in heaven. Each particle of the properties - i.e. each small piece of the host - is the whole Christ.

On the other hand, the properties of Christ's body in heaven cannot be completely absent from the host, since they express the substance there. Since the substance is in each particle of the host, the properties must be there accompanying them. This is called "concomitance". The "accidents" - size, shape, texture or molecular structure - of the Body of Christ are not present in a three-dimensional way by filling space, but in the manner of a substance without actual extension. Since the whole Christ present in heaven becomes physically present without any actual extension, the consecrated host is truly the bread of angels which they adore now. The altar becomes heaven with the adoration of the mystic lamb in the Apocalypse present to us. The altar becomes the place where all the works Christ did on earth become present to us. Yet heaven does not move; the bread and wine are changed wholly into the lamb who exists there now.

> Lo! the angel's food is given
> To the pilgrim who has striven;
> See the children's bread from heaven,
> Which on dogs may not be spent.

Christ instituted this sacrament precisely so that we, wayfarers and pilgrims, could share fully in the mystery of his atonement. This is a true memorial or <u>anamnesis</u>. He said, "Do this in memory of me." Yet, this is not just a play re-enacted. It is a true participation in the whole interior drama of his perfect obedience on the Cross. "The Eucharist is thus a sacrifice because it *re-presents* (makes present) the sacrifice of the cross, because it is its *memorial* and because it *applies* its fruit."[242] This begins in Christ's association of the Apostles with his Atonement at the Last Supper. For this reason, all Catholic accounts of the Passion begin not with the Agony, but with the Supper. The Supper and the Cross are intimately united. The sign and associated effects exist to plunge our own moral lives into the mystery of Christ's perfect obedience on the Cross.

> What he did at supper seated,
> Christ ordained to be repeated,
> His memorial never to cease:
> And his rule for guidance taking,
> Bread and wine we hallow making
> Thus our sacrifice of peace.
>
> Truth the ancient types fulfilling,
> Isaac bound, a victim willing
> Paschal lamb, its life blood spilling,
> manna to the fathers sent.

This change in the being of the bread is unique. It has similarities both to creation from nothing and to natural change, but it is also distinct from both. The change of transubstantiation is like creation and unlike natural change because in transubstantiation there is no subject which receives the change common to both the Body of Christ and the bread. Even the ultimate matter of the bread changes to the body of Christ. It is unlike creation and like natural change in two respects. First, it involves a real change. Creation is not a change. One thing does not become another; something comes to be where nothing existed before. In natural change there is a subject of the change, but this is not true in creation. In other words, in all other change, something, a subject, remains the same after the change. In natural change, the matter remains the same. This is not so in transubstantiation. In this change, the subject is the unchanging appearances of bread and wine. The properties are the medium of the change.

According to the Catholic faith, then, after the priest recites the words of institution, every facet and part of Christ is physically present, and really so, in the Host (the Victim). Not every part is present in the same way, though. Some parts are present as entailed in the sign, others are present by natural accompaniment. For example, in the consecration of the Host, only the body becomes present by sacramental sign. The words which induce the change are "This is my body", so only the body becomes present. The same is true of the wine.

Yet, by natural accompaniment, whatever is present to the body or blood in heaven is now present in the whole Christ on the altar. Body includes blood and vice versa. This is why, for all but the priest who confects the sacrifice, the reception of one species is sufficient to receive the whole reality. Because the body and blood are united to each other as well as to the soul and divinity, each includes the other and the soul and divinity. Had the Eucharist been celebrated during the time Christ was in the tomb, the body and blood would have been joined to the divinity but not to the soul, as the soul was separated from the body.

Here beneath these signs are hidden
Priceless things to sense forbidden
Signs, not things are all we see:
Blood is poured and flesh is broken
Yet in either wondrous token
Christ entire we know to be.

As the body becomes present in substance, so do all the things present in the body: i.e. bones, nerves and everything else. Yet the quantity, which is a true accident of bread, is not converted into the measurable quantity which expresses the bones, nerves and everything else of Christ in heaven; that would be cannibalism. The body and blood are not separate really; they are only separate by sign, and this is the sacramental expression of the sacrifice. The whole Christ present under two appearances stand as a memorial of his sacrifice when the body and blood existed in a separate state by death and allows us as the faithful to nourish our bodies and spirits with the nourishment of Christ.

> When the sacrament is broken,
> Doubt not but believe 'tis spoken
> That each sever'd outward token
> doth the very whole contain.
> Nought the precious gift divides,
> Breaking but the sign betides
> Jesus still the same abides,
> still unbroken does remain.

Every facet of the mystery of his body and blood becomes ours by natural accompaniment. His death becomes ours; his life becomes ours; his body mingles with ours, and as it is resurrected, prepares us for resurrection; the accepted obedience of his soul becomes ours; if we are open to it, his love becomes ours.

The substance of Christ's body is present in the sign, but the dimensions are present by accompaniment. His body therefore exists in the sacrament under the dimensions or appearances of the sign, not as dimensions of a body existing in the place containing them. If one could miraculously divide the quantity of the dimensions contained in the place of the resurrected body, for example, the finger from the hand of the resurrected Christ, he would have two pieces of the body, namely a finger and a hand; the substance would be divided. But in the Eucharist, when one breaks the appearances (the host), the whole substance (the Body of Christ) remains under each appearance. As long as the appearance is that of bread, the substance remains in it.

Thus, when I divide the Host, I do not have two parts of Christ's body, but two entire bodies of Christ. Christ's body is not localized in a place in its physical dimensions. If it were, Christ could not be in two places whole and entire at the same time. Yet, by this miraculous change of transubstantiation, in each place where the appearances exist, the whole Christ is there physically working his effect. This was mystically conveyed in sign at the multiplication of the loaves.

> Whoso of this food partakes,
> Does not rend the Lord nor breaks;
> Christ is whole to all that taste:
> Thousands are, as one, receivers,
> One, as thousands of believers,
> Eats of him who cannot waste.

The accidents, i.e. the bread and wine, are preserved in their own existence without a real subject. They express the body of Christ, but do not contain it. They therefore behave as they did before the change. The accidents can be divided or even corrupted. If the accidents of wine are corrupted, then the presence of Christ ceases and the being becomes what it would have had wine become corrupted, for example, vinegar.

The miraculous character of this substantial change occurs merely because the priest repeats the words of Christ. In this case, he speaks in the Person of Christ, not in his own person as minister. In all the other sacraments, the priest speaks in his own person, as minister (*ex persona ministr*i) saying "I baptize", "I confirm", and "I anoint". In this sacrament alone, he speaks directly in the person of Christ (*ex persona Christ capitis*) because this sacrament is not only the power of Christ, but is Christ himself. "This is My Body; This is My Blood." For this reason, it is more than just bad taste for the priest to dress, act or speak as though he were "Father X" speaking. He is Christ speaking and merely brings Christ present. This is the Real Presence with capital letters.

> This presence is called 'real' not in an exclusive sense, as if the other kinds of presence were not real, but 'par excellence', because it is a substantial presence by which Christ, the God-man, whole and entire becomes present.[243]

These other presences of Christ must be distinguished from the Real Presence. Christ is present in creation, in a sunset and a tree because as God he causes them, but not as though he were a part of the being of the sunset and the tree. God is an efficient, final and exemplary cause. He is not a form among forms though, since he is infinite and he is not a material cause, the potential of all things to be, since he has no potential. He is all. Christ is in my neighbor by image since all men have a soul. If my neighbor is in the state of grace, Christ is present in him as an accidental quality. I do not genuflect and adore my neighbor. I do genuflect and adore the host as God. Christ is present in his own flesh by the grace of the Hypostatic Union, which can never be lost. He is present in Person in his human nature. He is present in the Church as the head of his Mystical Body, but this is because he gives grace to the members. He is present in all the other sacraments because they bring grace to man by his power. He is Really Present in the Eucharist, by substance. This is unique and related to his presence by Hypostatic Union.

Since the whole purpose and effect of this sacrament is our union with the whole mystery of Christ, including his Mystical Body, the Church, one must be morally prepared to receive it. The more one practices the infused and theological virtues and enters into contemplative union with the Trinity, the more fruit this sacrament will bear in life. Those who are prepared are infused, like wax into wax, into the life of Christ and the Trinity. Since we must live a supernatural life to nourish the image of God in us and prepare for heaven, the food of Christ is necessary. Yet, just as one who is sick cannot really enjoy the taste of healthy food, so one who is in mortal sin cannot receive or enjoy the fruits of this sacrament. Moral preparation is absolutely necessary.

> Bad and good the feast are sharing,
> Of what divers ends preparing,
> Endless death or endless life.
> Life to these, to those damnation
> See how like participation
> Is with unlike issues rife.

Such is the great miracle of transubstantiation. By this change, both like and unlike creation and like and unlike nature, Christ himself becomes present to feed us with the moral value of his atonement and to prepare us morally and physically to live with him in resurrection forever. It is sad to read surveys which state that only 30% of Catholics still believe in this mystery. It is sad to see the precious Blood poured down the sink and patens unpurified. It is sad to see flagons of wine and crystal goblets consecrated as though all that were being done was our rehearsal of a love feast. All of these abuses arise from a bad metaphysics, in which all is reduced to appearances, and from a subjective celebration of humanity, in which all is horizontal. But Vatican II, Pope Paul VI, Pope John Paul II and the Catechism of the Catholic Church continue to affirm the opposite of these abuses: the great mystery of transubstantiation. The Eucharist is the food for "man fully alive"!

> True bread, good shepherd, tend us,
> Jesus, of your love befriend us,
> You refresh us, you defend us,
> Your eternal goodness send us

In the land of life to see.

You who all things can and know,
Who on earth such food bestowest,
Grant us with your saints though lowest
Where the heavenly feast you show,
Fellow heirs and guests to be. Amen.
ALLELUIA!

NOTES

[1] "Gloria enim Dei vivens homo, vita autem hominis visio Dei." St. Irenaeus, Adversus haereses, 4, 20, 7: PG 7/1, 1037. Cited by Catechism of the Catholic Church, n. 294.

[2]"Dignitatis humanae eximia ratio in vocatione hominis ad communionem cum Deo consistit. The Catechism of the Catholic Church (henceforth CCC), n. 27, cf. Gaudium et Spes, 19.

[3]CCC n. 30.

[4] Cf., for example, "For there exists in man a natural desire (naturale desiderium) of knowing the cause when he observes an effect. Wonder in men arose from this. If therefore the intellect of the reasoning creature could not arrive at the first cause of things, the desire of nature will remain in vain. Thus it must simply be conceded, that the Blessed see the essence of God." Summa Theologiae, I, 12, 1, ad corp. Cf. Also for example, Summa contra Gentiles, III, cc 25, 50, 54 (n. 2311 etc.); In II Sententiae. D. 23, q. 2, a. 1, objection 4 and 5; In Evang. Ioan, c. lect. 11 (n. 212 in the Marietti edition); In Evang. Matt. C.5 ver 10 (n. 434); ST, I-II, 3, 8; ST, I, 104; De Virtutibus in Communi, a. 10; In Immortalitate animae, One article, 4, sed contra.

[5] "Natura non largitur ad inclinationem aliquid ad quod tota vis natura perducere nequid." Cajetan, Commentary on the Summa Theologiae, I-II, 3, 8.

[6] "Haec glossa destruit textum, est tortuosa." Quoted in the Letters of Etienne Gilson to Henri de Lubac, (San Francisco: Ignatius Press, 1988), 101, note 3.

[7] Ludwig Ott, Fundamentals of Catholic Dogma, (Rockford, Illinois: Tan Books, 1974) 106.

[8] "Quando ergo ex propria ratione, adiutus divina gratia, apprehendit aliquod speciale bonum, ut suam beatitudinem, in quo vere sua beatitudo consistit, tunc meretur, non ex hoc quod appetit beatitudinem quam naturaliter appetit, sed ex hoc quod appetit hoc speciale quod non naturaliter appetit, ut visionem Dei, in quo tamen secundum rei veritatem sua beatitudo consistit." De Veritate, 22, 7, ad corp. There are many other interesting texts where the natural desire seems to be denied: e.g. ST I-II, 114, 3, objection 3; ST I-II, 114.

[9] Cf. Also, In III Sent. d. 27, q. 2, .a. 2, ad 4; In IV Sent. d. 43, q. 1, a. 4, qla. 3, 2, sc.; In II Sent. d. 12, q. 1, ad 1; In III Sent. D. 27, q. 2, a. 3, ad 4; In III Sent. D. 27, q. 2, a. 3, ad 5; In III Sent. D. 26, q. 1, ad 2.

[10] "Ecclesia symbolismum sermonis bibilici authentice sub Novi Testamenti et Traditionis luce interpretans, docet primos nostros parentes, Adamum et Evam, in statu sanctitatis et iustitiae originalis constitutos esse. Haec sanctitatis originalis gratia erat participatio vitae divinae." CCC n. 375. Cf. Council of Trent, Session 5, Decree on Original Sin, canon 1: DS 1511; Vatican II, Lumen Gentium, 2.

[11] Henri de Lubac, Augustinianism and Modern Theology, translated by Lancelot Sheppard (New York: Herder and Herder, 1969).

[12] Henri de Lubac, The Mystery of the Supernatural, translated by Rosemary Sheed (New York: Herder and Herder, 1967).

[13] Etienne Gilson, Letters of Etienne Gilson to Henri de Lubac, translated by Mary Emily Hamilton (San Francisco: Ignatius Press, 1988), 92.

[14] Henri de Lubac, The Mystery of the Supernatural (New York: Herder and Herder, 1967) 105.

[15] Ibid., 124.

[16] Ibid.

[17] Karl Rahner, "Concerning the Relationship of Nature and Grace," Theological Investigations, v. 1 (Baltimore: Helicon Press, 1963), 297-318.

[18] Ibid.

[19] Ibid. 313-314.

[20] Patrick J. Burke, "Conceptual Thought in Rahner", Gregorianum 75/1 (1994), 92.

[21] "Beatitudines naturali felcitatis respondent desiderio. ... Beatitudines scopum detegunt existentiae humanae, ultimum actuum humanorum finem: Deus nos ad Suam propriam vocat beatitudinem. Haec vocatio ad unumquemque dirigitur personaliter ... Novum Testamentum, ut beatitudinem insigniat, ad quam Deus hominiem vocat, pluribus utitur expressionibus: Adventu regni Dei; visione Dei ..." CCC 1718, 1719, 1720

[22] "Alii veram 'gratuitatem' ordinis supernaturalis corrumpunt, cum autument Deum entia intellectu praedita condere non posse, quin eadem ad beatificam visionem ordinet et vocet." Pius XII, Humani Generis, DS 3891 [2318]

[23] "E' una INCLINAZIONE: l'ordinazione della potenza al suo atto, al suo oggetto, la tendenze." Fr. Quintin Turiel, O.P. Il problema del destino umano in San Tommaso, class notes, Ponticial University of St. Thomas Aquinas in Urbe, 1984/85. All the articles of Fr. Turiel have been very influential in my ideas on this and many other subjects. The reader could profit greatly by availing himself of these jewels of Thomistic thought.

[24] "The appetite of form is not some act of matter, but a certain disposition of matter to form, according to which it is in potency to it.": Appetitus formae non est aliqua actio materiae, sed quaedam habitudo materiae ad formam, secundum quod est in potentia ad ipsam." Thomas Aquinas, De Potentia, 4, 1, ad 2, sed contra.

[25] "Proposuit igitur primo, quod omnibus hominibus naturaliter desiderium inest ad sciendum. Cuius ratio potest est triplex: Primo quidem, quia unaquaeque res naturaliter appetit perfectionem sui. Unde et materia dicitur appetere formam, sicut imperfectum appetit suam perfectionem. Cum igitur intellectus, a quo, homo est id quod est, in se consideratus sit in potentia omnia, nec in actum eorum reducatur nisi per scientiam, quia nihil est eorum quae sunt, ante intellegere, ...; sic naturaliter unusquisque desiderat scientiam sicut materia formam." Thomas Aquinas, In Metaphysicorum, I, l. 1, nn. 1-2.

[26] "Naturaliter inest omnibus hominibus desiderium cognoscendi causas eorum quae videntur: unde propter admirationem eorum quae videbantur, quorum causae latebant, homines primo philosophari coeperunt, invenientes autem causam quiescebant. Nec sistit inquisitio quousque perveniatur ad primam causam: et tunc perfecte nos scire arbitramur quando primam causam cognoscimus. Desiderat igitur homo naturaliter cognoscere primam causam quasi ultimum finem. Prima autem omnium causa Deus est. Est igitur ultimus finis hominis cognoscere Deum." Thomas Aquinas, Summa contra Gentiles (henceforth SCG), III, 25, n. 2065.

[27] "Illa igitur cognitio Dei essentialiter est ipsa felicitas, qua habita non restabit alicuius scibilis desideranda cognitio. Talis autem non est cognitio quam philosophi per demonstrationes de Deo habere potuerunt: quia adhuc, illa cognitione habita, alia desideramus scire,

quae per hanc cognitionem nondum sciuntur. Non est igitur in tali cognitione Dei felicitas." Thomas Aquinas, SCG, III, 39, n. 2172.

[28] "Amplius. Per felicitatem, cum sit ultimus finis, naturale desiderium quietatur. Cognitio autem fidei non quietat desiderium, sed magis autem ipsum accendit: quia unusquisque desiderat videre quod credit. Non est igitur in cognitione fidei ultima hominis felicitas." Thomas Aquinas, SCG, III, 40, n. 2178.

[29] "Omne enim quod est imperfectum in aliqua specie, desiderat consequi perfectionem speciei illius. ... Praedicta autem cognitio quam substantiae separatae habent de deo, non cognoscentes ipsius substantiam, est imperfecta cognitionis species ... unde et praecipuum in cognitione alicuius rei est scire de ea quid est. Ex hac igitur cognitione quam habent substantiae separatae non quiescit naturale desiderium, sed incitatur magis ad divinam substantiam videndam." Thomas Aquinas, SCG, III, 50, n. 2276.

[30] "Ex cognitione effectuum incitatur desiderium ad cognoscendum causam: unde homines philosophari incoeperunt causes rerum inquirentes. Non quiescit igitur sciendi desiderium, naturaliter omnibus substantiis inditum, nisi, cognitis substantiis effectuum, etiam substantiam causae cognoscant. Per hoc igitur quod substantiae separatae cognoscunt omnium rerum quarum substantias vident, esse Deum causam, non quiescit desiderium naturale in ipsis, nisi etiam ipsius Dei substantiam videant." Thomas Aquinas, SCG, 50 n. 2277.

[31] "Videmus autem quod videntes quia est aliquid, naturaliter scire desiderant propter quid. Ergo et cognoscentes an est aliquid, naturaliter scire desiderant quid est ipsum, quod est intelligere eius substantiam. Non igitur quietatur naturale sciendi desiderium in cognitione Dei qua scitur de ipso solum quia est." Thomas Aquinas, SCG, 50, n. 2278.

[32] "Nihil finitum desiderium intellectus quietare potest. ... Non igitur intellectus substantiae separatae quiescit per hoc quod cognoscit substantias creatas quantumcumque eminentes, sed adhuc naturali desiderio tendit ad intelligendum substantiam quae est altitudinis infinitae, ut in primo libro ostensum est de substantia divina." Thomas Aquinas, SCG, 50, n. 2279.

[33] "Sicut naturale desiderium inest omnibus intellectualibus naturis ad sciendum, ita inest eis naturale desiderium ignorantiam seu nescientiam pellendi. Substantiae separatae ... cognoscunt, praedicto cognitionis modo, substantiam Dei esse supra se et supra

omne id quod ab eis intelligitur: et per consequens sciunt divinam substantiam sibi esse ignotam. Tendit igitur naturale ipsorum desiderium ad intelligendum divinam substantiam." Thomas Aquinas, SCG, 50, n. 2280.

[34] Quanto aliquid est fini propinquius, tanto maiori desiderio tendit ad finem. ... Intellectus autem substantiarum separatarum propinquiores sunt divinae cognitioni quam noster intellectus. ... Multo magis substantiae separatae hoc naturaliter desiderant. Non igitur in cognitione Dei praedicta earum desiderium quietatur." Thomas Aquinas, SCG, 50, n. 2281.

[35] "Erubescant igitur qui felicitatem hominis, tam altissime sitam, in infimis rebus quaerunt." Thomas Aquinas, SCG, III, 50, n. 2283.

[36] I am indebted for this image as well as much of the substance of this chapter to the teaching and ideas of Fr. Quintin Turiel, O.P.

[37] "Similiter etiam est praeter rationem. Inest enim homini naturale desiderium cognoscendi causam, cum intuetur effectum; et ex hoc admiratio in hominibus consurgit. Si igitur intellectus rationalis creaturae pertingere non possit ad primam causam rerum, remanebit inane desiderium naturae. Unde simpliciter concedendum est quod beati Dei essentiam videant." Thomas Aquinas, ST, I, 12, ad corp.

[38] "Quamvis enim homo naturaliter inclinetur in finem ultimum, non tamen potest naturaliter illum consequi, sed solum per gratiam ..." Thomas Aquinas, In Boeth. De Trinitate, 6, 4, ad 5.

[39] "Nec differt, quantum ad hoc, sive respondeat passivo principio activum principium in natura respectu ultimae perfectionis, scilicet formae; sive respectu dispositionis quae est necessitas ad formam ultimam, sicut est in generatione hominis secundum positionis fidei, vel etiam de omnibus aliis secundum opinionem Platonis et Avicennae." Thomas Aquinas, Comm. Super Sententias, IV, d. 43, 1, 1, qla. 3, ad corp.

[40] "Et ideo ille effectus qui immediate est a deo tantum, et tamen inest recipienti ordo naturalis ad recipiendum illum effectum non per alium modum quam per istum, non erit miraculosus; sicut patet de infusione animae rationalis. Et similiter est de iustificatione impii: quia ordo naturalis inest animae ad iustitiae rectitudinem consequendam." Thomas Aquinas, In Comm. Super Sententias, IV, d. 17, 1, 5, ad corp.

[41] Cf. Thomas Aquinas, ST, I-II, 113, 3, ad corp.

[42] "Infelix homo qui scit omnia illa (scilicet creaturas), te autem nescit; beatus autem qui te scit, etiam si illa nesciat. Qui vero te et illa novit, non propter illa beatior est, sed propter te solum beatus." Augustine, Confessiones, V, 4, (PL 32, 708), quoted in Thomas Aquinas, ST, I, 12, 8, ad 4.

[43] "[...] est in horizonte, aeternitatis inferius et supra tempus." Thomas Aquinas, Liber de Causis, II, 2, n. 61.

[44] "rottura", Ibid., 76.

[45] Immanual Kant, Critique of Pure Reason, Introduction, Section II.

[46] "[Kant] 1) ha tolto l'essenza stessa della vita etica della sfera dell'esperienza empirica della persona e l'ha trasferita nella sfera extraempirica, noumenica; 2) in un solo e unico elemento psicologico, vale a dire nel sentimento del rispetto per la legge, ha cristallizzato l'intera esperienza etica del soggetto personale." Ibid., 78.

[47] John Paul II, Veritatis Splendor, n. 49.

[48] Ibid.

[49] Paul VI, Humanae Vitae, n. 7; John Paul II, Original Unity of Man and Woman (Boston, Massachusetts: St. Paul Editions, 1981), 173.

[50] Ibid.

[51] Pope John Paul II, Original, 57.

[52] "Corporeality and sexuality are not completely identified. Although the human body in its normal constitution bears within it the signs of sex and is, by its nature, male and female, the fact, however, that man is a 'body' belongs to the structure of the personal subject more deeply than the fact that he is in his somatic constitution also male and female." John Paul II, Original, 62.

[53] John Paul II, Splendor, n. 48. The Latin expressions in this text are references both to the early Church councils of Vienne and Fifth Lateran and to Gaudium et Spes in Vatican II, "Corpore et anima unus, homo per ipsam suam corporalem condicionem elementa mundi materialis in se colligit, ita ut, per ipsum, fastigium suum attingant et ad liberam Creatoris laudem vocem attolant."

[54] Catechism of the Catholic Church, n. 365.

[55] "Era caratteristica di Cartesio la divisione dell'uomo in sostanza estese, cioè corpo, e sostanza pensante, cioè anima - restando ambedue in un rapporto parallelo e non creando un tutto unico, un

unico sostanziale compositum humanum." Karol Wojtyla, I Fondamenti dell'Ordine Etico, "Il personalismo tomista," (Vatican City: Libreria Editrice Vaticana, 1980), 145. These articles have not been translated into English, so all translations in this articles will be my own.

56 "Vivo dunque me stesso, la mia propria persona, come causa efficiente del bene o del male della mia propria persona." Wojtyla, Fondamenti, "Il problema del distacco dell'esperienza dall'atto nell'etica nel contesto del pensiero di Kant e Scheler", 69.

57 "È per questo che san Tommaso. seguendo la concezione di Aristotele, lascia piuttosto da parte tutti gli altri coefficienti empirici, e si occupa innanzitutto del suo carattere essenziale, cioè dell'attualizzazione della volontà connessa sia con l'azione della ragion pratica che con l'azione dei fattori emotive, ed infine di tutti gli altri fattori che, grazie all'appartenenza al compositum umanum (sic), partecipano all'atto etico." Ibid., 70.

58 "Quando Scheler si trova di fronte a quell'insieme empirico costituito dall'esperienza etica dell'uomo, afferma immediatamente che quest'esperienza ha il carattere dell'atto della persona." Wojtyla, Problema, 80-81.

59 Ibid.

60 "La cosa più importante invece è il fatto che questi valori non costituiscono l'oggetto del volere." Ibid, 83.

61 "Scheler ha fondato l'intera esperienza etica su elementi secondari, perchè l'aveva privata della spina dorsale della volontà." Ibid, 86.

62 "Affermiamo dunque che in ambedue le concezioni, quelle di Kant e quella di Scheler, così importanti per la storia dell'etica, insieme al distacco della vecchia concezione dell'atto etico si è avuta una certa deformazione dell'esperienza etica stessa." Ibid, 88.

63 "Il personalismo tomista", Karol Wojtla, I fondamenti, 141-152.

64 "persona est rationalis naturae individua substantia." Wojtyla, personalismo, 143.

65 "Le facoltà in cui si esprime e attualizza la spiritualità dell'anima, e quindi la spiritualità dell'uomo, sono la ragione e la libera volontà. Esse costituiscono, in un certo senso, i principali mezzi di realizzazione della persona umana; in base alla loro azione si modella l'intera personalità psicologica e morale. Queste facoltà non sono però le uniche dell'anima umana. Poiché essa è la forma

sostanziale del corpo . . . San Tommaso se ne rende conto perfettamente e caratterizza la spiritualità dell'uomo conformemente alla realtà. Nella sua concezione è questa una spiritualità tale a cui in somma misura è conforme l'unificazione sostanziale con la corporeità e quindi con la sensitività." Wojtyla, Ibid, 144-145.

[66] "Quindi in san Tommaso vidiamo benissimo la persona nella sua obietiva esistenza e azione, ma è difficile scorgervi le esperienze vissute della persona." Wojtyla, personalismo, 147.

[67] "L'uomo rappresenta un compositum spirituale-materiale, razionale-sensitivo, quindi agiscono in lui anche le energie dell'amore sensuale, ma gli è comunque proprio l'amore spirituale." Wojtyla, Ibid, 149.

[68] Karol Wojtyla, Love and Responsibility (London, Collins: 1981), 41.

[69] John Paul II, Original Unity of Man and Woman, (Boston: St. Paul Publications, 1981, 109.

[70] Ibid, 111.

[71] Ibid., 117.

[72] Ibid., 123.

[73] Ibid., 142.

[74] Ibid., 144.

[75] Ibid., 138.

[76] Wojtyla, personalismo, 143.

[77] "*Collegium* non intelligitur sensu *stricte iuridico*, scilicet de coetu aequalium, qui potestatem suam praesidi suo demandarent, sed de coetu stabili, cuius structura et auctoritas ex Revelatione deduci debent." Nota Explicitiva Praevia, Lumen Gentium, 1, 1964.

[78] C.S. Lewis, The Screwtape Letters (New York: The Macmillan Company, 1973), 161, 170.

[79] David Blankenhorn, Fatherless America (New York: Harper Collins, 1995), 67.

[80] National Catholic Register, 27 November 1983. Cited from Anne Roche Muggeridge, The Desolate City (San Francisco: Harper and Row, 1986), 143.

[81] "Deus est in omnibus rebus, non quidem sicut pars essentiae, vel sicut accidens, sed sicut agens adest ei in quod agit."" Thomas Aquinas, Summa Theologiae (henceforth ST), I, 8, 1, ad corp.

80Manfred Hauke, Women in the Priesthood (San Francisco: Ignatius Press, 1988), 225. The same reasoning can be employed in the celebrated assertion of Pope John Paul I in the Angelus message of September 10, 1978, "We are the object of God's everlasting love. ... He is our Father, still more, he is also a mother to us."

[83] "Incorporalia non sunt in loco per contactum quantitatis dimensivae, sicut corpora; sed per contactum virtutis." Thomas Aquinas, ST, I, 8, 2, ad 1.

[84] CCC n. 239.

[85] "Cum igitur Deus sit extra totum ordinem creaturae, et omnes creaturae ordinentur ad ipsum, e non e converso, manifestum est quod, creaturae realiter referuntur ad ipsum Deum; sed in Deo non est aliqua realis relatio eius ad creaturas, sed secundum rationem tantum, inquantum creaturae referunter ad ipsum." Thomas Aquinas, ST, I, 13, 7, ad corp.

[86] CCC n. 240.

[87] St. Gregory Nazianzus, MG 36, 96.

[88] Thomas Aquinas, ST, I, 29, 4.

[89] Cf. Thomas Aquinas, ST, I, 34, 3, ad corp.

[90] "[...] in semine hominis esse quiddam divinum [...]," Aristotle, On the Generation of Animals, II, 3. Quoted by Thomas Aquinas, De Malo, 15, 2, ad corp..

[91] Catechism of the Catholic Church, n. 1750.

[92] CCC, n. 1755.

[93] Richard McCormick, S.J., "Killing the Patient", The Tablet, 30 October (1993), 1410-1411.

[94] Cf. McCormick above.

[95]CCC, n. 1751.

[96] CCC, n. 1756.

[97] John Paul II, Veritatis Splendor, n. 44.

[98] Ibid., n. 46.

[99] Augustine, Ennaratio in Psalmum XCIX, 7: CCL 39, 1397. Quoted by John Paul II, in Veritatis Splendor, n. 87.

[100] Karl Rahner, Foundations of the Christian Faith (New York: Seabury Press, 1978), 450.

[101] Bernhard Haring, "A Distrust that Wounds", The Tablet, 23 October, 1993, p. 1378.

[102] Patrick J. Burke, "Conceptual Thought in Karl Rahner", Gregorianum, v. 75, 1 (1994) 92.

[103] Karl Rahner, S.J. Theological Investigations, "On the Question of a Formal Existential Ethics", v. II, translated by Karl H. Charger (Baltimore: Helicon Press, 1963) 226.

[104] Ibid., 228.

[105] Ibid. 228.

[106] Ibid., see footnote 3.

[107] C.S. Lewis, The Screwtape Letters (New York: Macmillan Publishing Company, 1982), 81-2.

[108] Thomas Aquinas, Summa Theologiae, I, 18, 3, ad corp.

[109] Pseudo-Dionysius the Areopagite, On the Divine Names, 6, 1-3: PG 3, 856-857. Quoted in John Paul II, The Gospel of Life, n. 84.

[110] Peter Kreeft, A Summa of the Summa (San Francisco: Ignatius Press, 1990), note 50, 95.

[111] Dionysius, Names in Gospel of Life, n. 84.

[112] Gregory of Nyssa, De Hominis Opificio, 4: PG 44, 136; quoted in John Paul II, Life, n. 52.

[113] ". . . in semine hominis esse quiddam divinum." Thomas Aquinas, De Malo, 15, 2, ad corp.

[114] Dionysius, Names in John Paul II, Gospel of Life, 92.

[115] John Paul II, Life, n. 2.

[116] John Paul II, Life, n. 4.

[117] John Paul II, n. 5.

[118] John Paul II, Life, n. 10.

[119] John Paul II, Life, n. 12.

[120] John Paul II, Life, n. 12.

[121] John Paul II, Life, n. 15.

[122] John Paul II, Life, n. 18.

[123] John Paul II, Life, n. 19.

[124] cf. "As Cardinal John Henry Newman, that outstanding defender of the rights of conscience forcefully put it: 'Conscience has rights because it has duties'." John Paul II, Veritatis Splendor, n. 34.

[125] Ibid., n. 32.

[126] John Paul II, Life, n.19.

[127] Ibid.

[128] Ibid.

[129] John Paul II, Life, n.23.

[130] "Quia iste clamat vindictam, sed sanguis Christi ibi clamat veniam." Thomas Aquinas, In Hebraeos, XII, lect. IV, n. 712.

[131] John Paul II, Life, n. 25.

[132] John Paul II, Life, n. 34.

[133] "Vita autem hominis vivens homo." Adversus Haereses, IV, 20, 7: Sch. 100/2, 648-649; John Paul II, Life, n. 34, note 23; The Catechism of the Catholic Church, n. 294.

[134] "Ut vita carnis anima est, ita beata vita hominis Deus est." Augustine, The City of God, 19, 26 (PL 41:656).

[135] "Vita autem hominis visio Dei": Adversus Haereses, IV, 20, 7: Sch 100/2, 648-649; The Catechism of the Catholic Church, n. 294.

[136] John Paul II, Ibid., n. 43.

[137] Ibid., n. 46.

[138] Ibid., n. 51.

[139] John Paul II, Life, nn. 57, 62 and 63.

[140] Ibid., 57.

[141] Ibid., n. 62.

[142] Ibid. n. 65.

[143] Ibid., n. 56.

[144] cf. The Catechism of the Catholic Church, nn. 2263-2267.

[145] John Paul II, Life, n. 55.

[146] John Paul II, Life, n. 52.

[147] St. Augustine, Ennaratio in Psalmum XCIX, 7: CCL 39, 1397 quoted in John Paul II, Vertitatis Splendor, n. 87.

[148] John Paul II, Life, n. 70.

[149] Ibid., n. 71.

[150] Ibid.

[151] Ibid., n. 73.

[152] St. Augustine, In Iohannis Evangelium Tractatus, 41, 10: CCL 36, 363; cf. John Paul II, Veritatis Splendor, 13 quoted in John Paul II, Life, 75.

[153] Ibid., n. 89.

[154] Ibid., n. 104.

[155] Ibid.

[156] Hymn "O God of Loveliness", St. Alphonsus Ligouri.

[157] John of the Cross, The Collected Works of St. John of the Cross, (Washington, D.C.: ICS Publications, 1973), 720.

[158] The Catechism of the Catholic Church, n. 1720.

[159] cf. for example, I-Man; Rahner, The Theology of Death and Ladislas Boros, The Mystery of Death.

[160] "In that in the face of which one has anxiety, the 'It is nothing and nowhere' becomes manifest. The obstinacy of the 'nothing and nowhere within-the-world' means as a phenomenon that the world as such is that in the face of which one has anxiety." Martin Heidegger, Being and Time, n. 40. Trans. John Macquarrie and Edward Robinson, (Harper and Row, Publishers; New York: 1962), 231.

[161] Mieczylaw A. Krapiec, I-Man, (New Britain, Conn.: Mariel Publications, 1983), 335.

[162] I-Man., 336.

[163] Heidegger, Being, n. 53, 266.

[164] Ladislas Boros, The Mystery of Death, (Herder and Herder: New York, 1965), 8.

[165] Mystery, 9.

[166] Ibid.

[167] Ibid.

[168] Ibid.

[169] Heidegger, Being, 306.

[170] Ibid., 310.

[171] Boros, Death, 165.

[172] Karl Rahner, On the Theology of Death, trans. C. H. Henkey, (New York: The Seabury Press, 1973), 18.

[173] Ibid., 19.

[174] John Damascene, De Fide Orthodoxa, 2, 4; Thomas Aquinas, In II Sent., d. 7, q. 1, a. 1; In IV Sent., d. 46, q. 1. a. 3; De Veritate, 24, 10, sc 4; Summa Theologiae, I, 64, 2.

[175] Rahner, Death, 30.

[176] Boros, Mystery of Death, 93.

[177] Boros, Mystery of Death 94.

[178] Rahner, Death, 32.

[179] Rahner, Death, 43.

[180] Ibid., 42.

[181] Karl Rahner, Death, 50.

[182] Rahner, Death, 40-41.

[183] Ibid, 41.

[184] Ibid. 43.

[185] Ibid., 58.

[186] Ibid., 59.

[187] Ibid.

[188] Ibid., 61.

[189] Ibid., 62.

[190] Ibid., 64.

[191] Ibid.

[192] Ibid.

[193] Ibid., 66.

[194] Cf. for example, "This consciousness (the beatific knowledge attributed to Christ) was Jesus' act of self-awareness, not a knowledge of an object but a knowledge of himself, of his divine person as subject. . . . So we cannot attribute to Jesus in his earthly life a state of glory which Scripture clearly excludes and which is clearly stated to have been merited by his death. . . . But the fullness of human beatitude was not given to Christ in his state of kenosis and was to be granted to him only as the crowning event of his sacrifice." Jean Galot, "Science et conscience de Jesus," Nouvelle Revue théologique 82 (1960), 113-31; also Theology Digest I (1964), 48-52. Cf. also, "The sufferings of Christ reported in the Gospels clearly indicate that he did not possess the beatific vision during his earthly life," Karl Rahner, "The Human Knowledge and Consciousness of Christ," Theology Digest 12 (1964), 53-5.

[195] Ibid., 69.

[196] Ibid., 71.

[197] Ibid., 70.

[198] Ibid., 71.

[199] Ibid.

[200] "Necessitas moriendi partim homini est ex natura, partim ex peccato," Thomas Aquinas, In III Sententiarum, d. 16, 1, 1, ad corp.

[201] "Naturale dicitur quod ex principiis naturae causatur. Naturae autem per se principia sunt forma et materia. Forma autem hominis est anima rationalis, quae de se est immortalis. Et ideo mors non est naturalis homini ex parte suae formae." Aquinas, ST, II-II, 164, 1, ad 1.

[202] "Hoc autem apparet per auctoritatem Aristotelis. Dicit enim in I De Anima, quod intellectus videtur substantia quaedam esse, et non corrumpi." Thomas Aquinas, Summa Contra Gentiles, II, c. 179, n. 1608. Cf. also "Unde videtur quod intellectus et omnis anima sit incorruptibilis, et quod debilitatio in eius operationibus non sit ex eo quod ipsa corrumpatur, sed ex eo quod debilitantur organa." Aquinas, Comm. In De Anima, I, l. 10, n. 163.

[203] "Mors est hominis natura, non poena." Aquinas, Comm. II Super Sententias, d. 30, 1, 1, obj. 1. Cf. Seneca, Ep. 9.

[204] Aristole, Metaphysics, I, 982b 11-15 and 983a 24.

[205] "Hoc igitur attendentes, quidam posuerunt quod nullus intellectus creatus essentiam Dei videre potest. . . . Similiter etiam est praeter rationem. Inest enim homini naturale desiderium cognoscendi causam, cum intuetur effectum; et ex hoc admiratio in hominibus consurgit. Si igitur intellectus rationalis creaturae pertingere non possit ad primam causam rerum, remanebit inane desiderium naturae. Unde simpliciter concedendum est quod beati Dei essentiam videant." Aquinas, ST, I, 12, 1, ad corp.

[206] Aquinas, SCG, III, c. 50.

[207] "Ut vita carnis anima est, ita beata vita hominis Deus est." Augustine, The City of God, 19, 26 (PL 41:656).

[208] I de Caelo et Mundo, c. 2 (29b 6-10). Cf. Thomas Aquinas, In IV Sent. d. 46, 1, 3, obj. 5; Suppl. 99, 1, obj. 5; d. 48, 2, 1, obj. 4; Suppl. 91, 1, obj. 4); In I de Caelo et Mundo, lect. 4 n. 49; Compendium Theologiae, I, c. 151; Q. Disputata de Anima, 1, ad 5; De Veritate, 24, 10, obj. 1.

[209] "el callejón sin salida". I am indebted for this idea and the general considerations in this part of the book to the extremely insightful article of Fr. Quintin Turiel, O.P., "¿Es La Resurreccion una verdad accesible a la Razon? Posicion de Sto. Tomas al Respecto," L'Anima nell'Antropologia di S. Tommaso d'Aquino, Edizioni Vivere In, Rome: 1987, 411.

[210] "Ad primum ergo dicendum quod Seneca et alii philosophi consideraverunt naturam humanam secundum ea quae ex principiis suis naturalibus ipsam consequuntur: statum enim illum primae conditionis scire non potuerunt, quem non nisi fides tenet; et ideo de morte non nisi sicut de naturali defectu locuti sunt; quamvis etiam naturalis defectus aliquo modo poena dici possit." Thomas Aquinas, In II Super Sententias, d. 30, 1, 1, ad 1.

[211] "Sed tamen in statu innocentiae donum quoddam a Deo gratis datum animae inerat, ut ipsa praeter modum aliarum formarum, secundum modum suum vitam indeficientem corpori largiretur, sicut ipsa incorruptibilis est, et non secundum modum corporis corruptibilem, quamdiu ipsa manebat deo subdita, et corpus ei omnino subdebatur, nec aliqua dispositio in corpore accidere poterat quae vivificationem animae impediret." Aquinas, In III Super Sententiarum, d. 16, 1, 1, ad corp.

[212] "Sed propter peccatum istud donum ablatum est; et ideo relicta est natura humana . . . in statu qui debetur ei ex natura suorum principiorum, secundum quod dictum est ei (Gen. III, 19): 'Terra es et in terram ibis.' Et ideo post peccatum, necessitas moriendi inest homini ex peccato, sicut ex removente prohibens, quod erat gratia innocentiae; ex natura autem materiae, sicut ex eo quod per se necessitatem mortis inducit." Ibid.

[213] ". . . per comparationem ad statum innocentiae." Ibid., ad 5.

[214] "Est autem hominis duplex mors et duplex vita. Una quidem mors est corporis per separationem ab anima; alia per separationem a Deo. . . . Similiter etiam per oppositum intelligitur duplex vita: una quidem corporis ab anima, quae dicitur vita naturae; alia a Deo, quae dicitur vita iustitiae, vel vita gratiae." Thomas Aquinas, Compendium Theologiae, c. 239.

[215] "A un callejón sin salida." Quintin Turiel, O.P., "¿Es la resurreccion una verdad accesible a la razon? Posicion de Sto. Tomas al respecto," L'Anima nell'Antropologia di S. Tommaso d'Aquino, Studia Universitatis S. Thomae in Urbe, v. 28 (Milan: Massimo, 1987), 407.

[216] "Et secundum hoc duplex est resurrectio: una corporis, qua anima iterato coniungitur corpori; alia spiritualis, qua iterum coniungitur Deo." Ibid.

[217] "While the 'beatitude' of this vision in Christ need not be experienced so nearly and immediately as something necessarily always 'beatifying'; after all, is it not conceivable that the vision may be undergone as a 'consuming fire' in certain situations proper to a 'viator'?", Karl Rahner, Theological Investigations, v. 1, (Baltimore: Helicon Press, 1963), 170, note 2. Cf. also Jean Galot, "Science et conscience de Jesus", Nouvelle Revue Théologique 82 (1960), 113-31.

[218] Rahner, Theology of Death, 61. For a more contemporary explanation of the same point, see, for example, "He (Jesus) went to his death knowing at least that it was the fate of a prophet, and he accepted his death in the light of his conviction that God would vindicate what he had said, done, and been. [...] It is readily admitted that this theological explanation is not the one operative in the magisterial documents under consideration [...] Even if one were to grant, however, that these documents do condemn the position presented here, and by Rahner and other Catholic theologians elsewhere, one would still have to raise the question of the authoritative status of such condemnations. [...] The word of God, as

proclaimed in the New Testament and as interpreted in the light of present theological principles, calls into question the apparent intent of the magisterial pronouncements of the question of the knowledge of Jesus." Richard McBrien, Catholicism (San Francisco: Harper, 1994) 555-557.

[219] Pius XII, Mystici Corporis, #75.

[220] CCC, #473.

[221] "No one takes my life from me. I have power to lay down my life and I have power to take it up again." John 10:18.

[222] Cf., for example, "Doubtless our Lord continues the psalm in silence. The fact that the words are a quotation removes the dogmatic difficulty. The psalm is not a cry of despair but, on the contrary, a hymn of supreme confidence in God despite profound suffering. As in our Lord's case the divine 'forsaking' in the psalm is no more than a poetical expression of acute physical and mental pain to which God has 'abandoned' his face without, however, having 'turned his face away', Ps. 21 (22), 2, 25." A Catholic Commentary on Holy Scripture, eds. Bernard Orchard, Edmund Sutcliffe, Reginald Fuller, and Ralph Russell, (New York: Thomas Nelson and Sons, 1953) 903.

[223] John Paul II, General Audience, November 30, 1988.

[224] For this section of the article, I am very much indebted to the former work cited of Richard T. A. Murphy, Abandonment, especially pages 187-8.

[225] Murphy, Abandonment, 188.

[226] Thomas Aquinas, ST, III, 50, 2, ad 1.

[227] The Roman Catechism, I, &, 7.

[228] Bertrand de Margerie, S.J. An Introduction to the History of Exegesis: St. Augustine, v. III (Petersham: St. Bede's Publications, 1982) 134, note 42.

[229] 1 Cor. 15: 54-56.

[230] CCC, #163.

[231] John of the Cross, The Living Flame of Love, st. 3, n. 18.

[232] J.P. De Caussade, Self-Abandoment to the Divine Providence, I, I, 1.

233 Elizabeth of the Trinity, The Complete Works, v. 1, translated by Sister Aletheia Kane (Washington, D.C., ICS Publications, 1984) 148.

234 "Quidam dixerunt quod nullus meretur absolute vitam aeternam, nisi per actum finalis gratiae; sed solum sub conditione, *si perseverat*. – Sed hoc irrationabiliter dicitur: quia quandoque actus ultimae gratiae non est magis meritorius, sed minus quam actus praecedentis, propter aegritudinis oppressionem. Unde dicendum quod actus caritatis meretur absolute vitam aeternam." Thomas Aquinas, ST, I-II, 114, 7, ad 3.

235 Catechism of the Catholic Church, n. 1682.

236 James Weisheipl, O.P. Friar Thomas d'Aquino (New York: Doubleday and Company, Inc. 1974) 326.

237 Aidan Nichols, The Holy Eucharist, (Dublin: Veritas, 1991) 59.

238 Ibid., 65.

239 Lanfranc, De Corpore et Sanguine Domini, 18, 19. Cited in Nichols, Eucharist, p. 138, note 10.

240 D.-S. 802.

241 Paul VI, Mysterium Fidei, n. 146.

242 CCC, #1366.

243 Paul VI, Mysterium Fidei.

About The Author

Fr. Brian Mullady, O.P., S.T.D. is a Catholic Priest and member of the Dominican Order. He has been a priest for 30 years. In that time, he has been variously a parish priest, high school teacher and college professor teaching at the University of San Francisco, the Angelicum University in Rome, the Pope's *alma mater*, and the University of St. Thomas in Houston. He has also authored a book which was published by the Pontifical Academy of St. Thomas in Rome through Vatican Press and numerous books and articles. He has had several TV and radio series on EWTN and WEWN respectively. He is a popular preacher and much sought after for parish missions and retreats. He is at present the head of the department of Systematic Theology at Holy Apostles Seminary in Cromwell, CT. He brings both his unique and varied experience in pastoral life and in the study and teaching of St. Thomas Aquinas to his written works.

Printed in the United States
17796LVS00003B/187-432

9 781403 399342